IQPuzzles

IQ Puzzles

ARCTURUS

ARCTURUS

This edition published in 2014 by Arcturus Publishing Limited
26/27 Bickels Yard, 151–153 Bermondsey Street,
London SE1 3HA

Copyright © Arcturus Holdings Limited

ISBN: 978-1-78404-030-7
AD004312NT

Typeset by MATS, Southend-on-Sea, Essex
Cover design by Maki Ryan

Printed in China

Prepare yourself for the ultimate test of your brain power! We've devised over 500 IQ puzzles to stretch your logical and lateral thinking abilities to the limit.

This book has been meticulously compiled from some of the most devious puzzles you've seen. Some will require keen mathematical skill, others an ability to recognise abstract patterns, but all our puzzles are supremely logical and can be solved with the right approach.

If you have a sharp mind, some of the answers to these puzzles will jump straight out of the page at you. However, others will require a bit more thought. Try not to rush for an answer straight away – have faith in your abilities and all will become clear – and don't feel tempted to have a peek at the answer page too soon. If you feel completely stumped by one particular puzzle, then move on and come back to it later – coming up with the solution to a later puzzle just might give you the inspiration you need!

But the idea of this book is not about right and wrong answers, it's about exercising your mind and flexing your mental muscles. With the right approach, you too can discover your IQ potential.

The large variety of puzzles here are designed to test your powers of lateral thinking and problem solving to the max! You'll have to be able to recognize patterns and sequences, spot similarities and differences and even pick your way through our convoluted mindbenders. The solutions to all the puzzles in this book are staring you right in the face – you just have to be looking at them in the right way!

So sit back, relax your body and let your brain take the strain – it's all a matter of logic.

Multiplication Table

×	1	2	3	4	5	6	7	8	9	10	11	12
1	1	2	3	4	5	6	7	8	9	10	11	12
2	2	4	6	8	10	12	14	16	18	20	22	24
3	3	6	9	12	15	18	21	24	27	30	33	36
4	4	8	12	16	20	24	28	32	36	40	44	48
5	5	10	15	20	25	30	35	40	45	50	55	60
6	6	12	18	24	30	36	42	48	54	60	66	72
7	7	14	21	28	35	42	49	56	63	70	77	84
8	8	16	24	32	40	48	56	64	72	80	88	96
9	9	18	27	36	45	54	63	72	81	90	99	108
10	10	20	30	40	50	60	70	80	90	100	110	120
11	11	22	33	44	55	66	77	88	99	110	121	132
12	12	24	36	48	60	72	84	96	108	120	132	144

Cube Numbers | Square Numbers

n	Cube Numbers	Square Numbers
1	1	1
2	8	4
3	27	9
4	64	16
5	125	25
6	216	36
7	343	49
8	512	64
9	729	81
10	1000	100
11	1331	121
12	1728	144
13	2197	169
14	2744	196
15	3375	225
16	4096	256
17	4913	289
18	5832	324
19	6859	361
20	8000	400

Numerical Values

#	Letter	Value
1	A	26
2	B	25
3	C	24
4	D	23
5	E	22
6	F	21
7	G	20
8	H	19
9	I	18
10	J	17
11	K	16
12	L	15
13	M	14
14	N	13
15	O	12
16	P	11
17	Q	10
18	R	9
19	S	8
20	T	7
21	U	6
22	V	5
23	W	4
24	X	3
25	Y	2
26	Z	1

Prime Numbers

2, 3, 5, 7, 11, 13, 17, 19, 23, 29

1
PUZZLE

What is missing in the last grid?

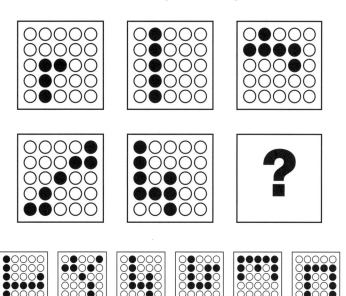

A   B   C   D   E   F

2
PUZZLE

What time should the missing watch read?

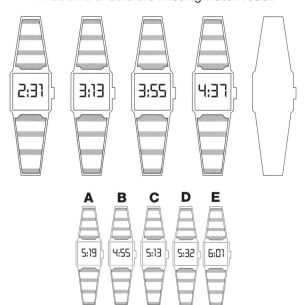

A   B   C   D   E

PUZZLE 3

Which circle replaces the question mark?

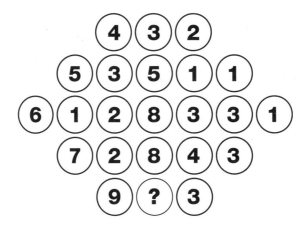

PUZZLE 4

Which number replaces the question mark and completes the puzzle?

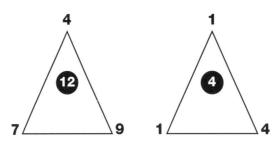

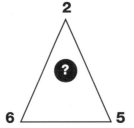

PUZZLE 5

Which letter replaces the question mark to end the sequence that starts in the top left segment of the circle?

Y   W

?   T

K   P

PUZZLE 6

Which number completes the puzzle?

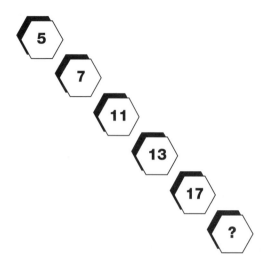

5
7
11
13
17
?

PUZZLE 7

Which letter replaces the question mark and completes the puzzle?

B

F

J

N

R

?

PUZZLE 8

Which number replaces the question mark and completes the puzzle?

?

9   25

4   36

1   81   64   49

1

9 PUZZLE

Which letter is missing from the lower middle hexagon?

 E
 M
 H

 N
 O
 A

 I
 ?
 D

10 PUZZLE

Which letter completes the puzzle?

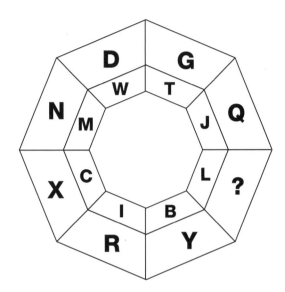

D   G
W   T
N   Q
M   J
X   C   L   ?
I   B
R   Y

11 PUZZLE

Which number is missing from the bottom triangle?

3
5
8
13
22
?

12 PUZZLE

Which number replaces the question mark and completes the puzzle?

7	3	6	2
2	8	5	4
1	1	2	4
4	2	1	?

PUZZLE 13

Which letter completes this puzzle?

PUZZLE 14

Which letter replaces the question mark to make this puzzle work?

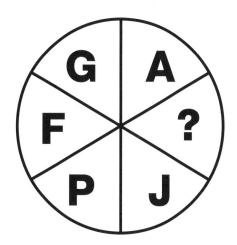

PUZZLE 15

Which number replaces the question mark and completes the puzzle?

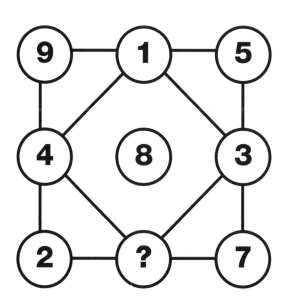

PUZZLE 16

Where should the minute hand be put on the bottom clock?

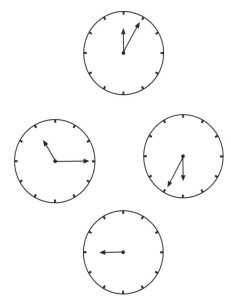

PUZZLE 17

What is missing from the last hexagon?

26 28 31 35 ?

PUZZLE 18

Which letter completes the puzzle?

B

C

E

G

?

PUZZLE 19

Which number replaces the question mark and completes the puzzle?

Square 1:
2 (top), 7 (left), 4 (right), 9 (bottom)

Square 2:
11 (top), 3 (left), 2 (right), 6 (bottom)

Square 3:
5 (top), 5 (left), 6 (right), 6 (bottom)

Square 4:
1 (top), 8 (left), 4 (right), ? (bottom)

PUZZLE 20

Which number replaces the question mark and completes the puzzle?

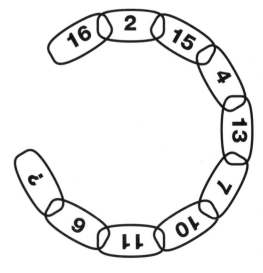

16 2 15 4 13 7 10 11 6 ?

14

PUZZLE 21

What is missing from the last circle?

9   8   4

2

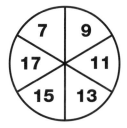 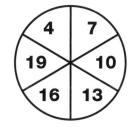 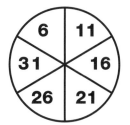

2   6   ?

PUZZLE 22

Which letter completes the puzzle?

I   F

?   E   C

E   G

PUZZLE 23

Which number replaces the question mark and completes the puzzle?

7	9
17	11
15	13

4	7
19	10
16	13

6	11
31	16
26	21

1	5
21	9
17	?

PUZZLE 24

Which letter replaces the question mark and completes the puzzle?

Z

S G

M D I

F E H ?

PUZZLE 25

Which letter is missing from the lower right hand circle?

A	C	G	I
E	Y	K	E
I	U	O	A
M	Q	S	?

PUZZLE 26

Which number replaces the question mark and completes the puzzle?

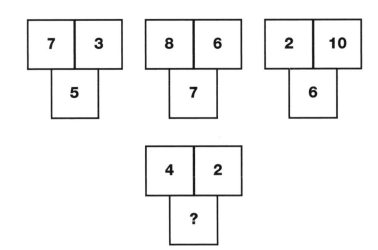

| 7 | 3 | | 8 | 6 | | 2 | 10 |
| 5 | | | 7 | | | 6 | |

| 4 | 2 |
| ? | |

PUZZLE 27

What is missing from the last square?

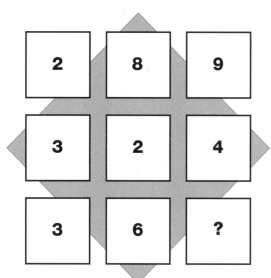

PUZZLE 28

Which numbers complete the puzzle?

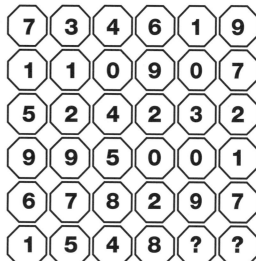

PUZZLE 29

Which number is the odd one out in each oval?

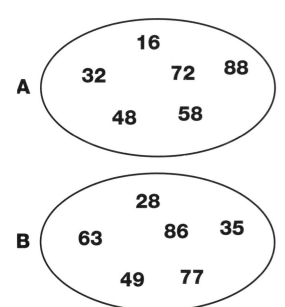

PUZZLE 30

Which letter replaces the question mark and completes the puzzle?

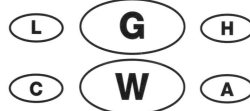

T E S T 1

17

PUZZLE 1

What is missing from the last segment?

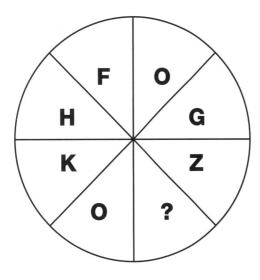

PUZZLE 2

Which letter completes the puzzle?

PUZZLE 3

Which tool will make the last scale balance?

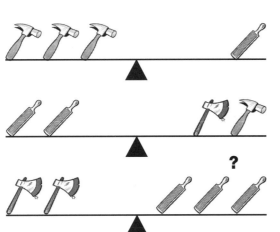

PUZZLE 4

Which number replaces the question mark and completes the puzzle?

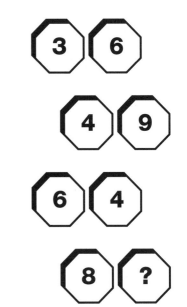

5
PUZZLE

What is missing from the lower middle circle?

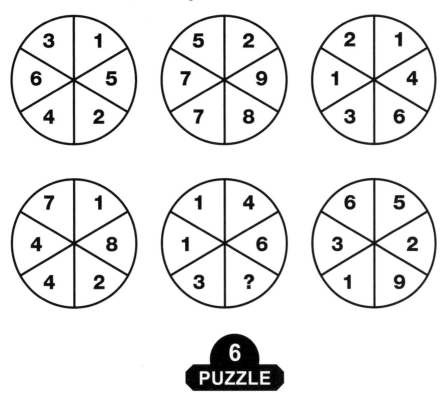

6
PUZZLE

Which letter replaces the question mark and completes the puzzle?

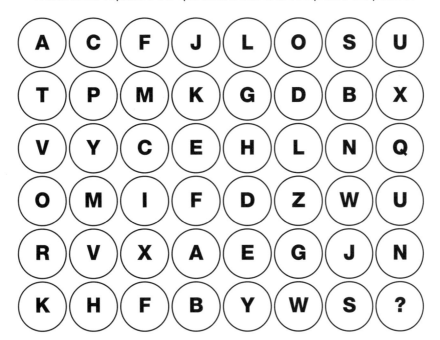

2

PUZZLE 7

What is missing from the bottom right hand circle?

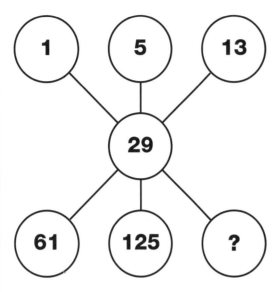

PUZZLE 8

Which letter completes the puzzle?

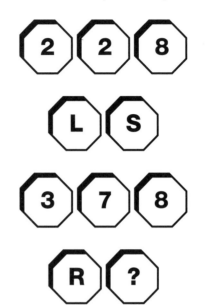

PUZZLE 9

Which number replaces the question mark and completes the puzzle?

| 6 | 9 | 15 | 27 | ? |

PUZZLE 10

Which number replaces the question mark and completes the puzzle?

10	
8	13
16	6
4	19
22	?

11 PUZZLE

What is missing from the last circle?

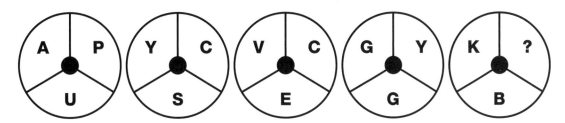

12 PUZZLE

Which number replaces the question mark and completes the puzzle?

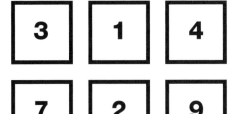

3	1	4
7	2	9
1	5	?

13 PUZZLE

Which letter completes the puzzle?

14 PUZZLE

Which number replaces the question mark and completes the puzzle?

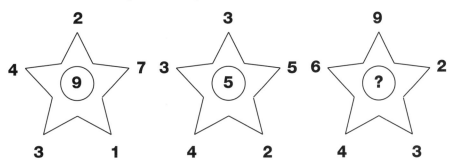

T E S T

 2

15 PUZZLE

What is missing from the last circle?

 2   7   17

 3   11   19

5   13   ?

16 PUZZLE

Which number completes the puzzle?

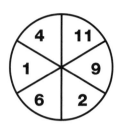

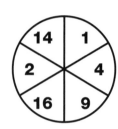

17 PUZZLE

Which letter replaces the question mark and completes the puzzle?

G	B	C
H	F	H
A	D	?

B   D   I   E   K

22

18 PUZZLE

Which four digit number is missing from the last oval?

195

383

575

763

955

?

19 PUZZLE

Which number completes the puzzle?

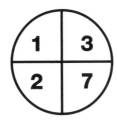

20 PUZZLE

Which letter replaces the question mark and completes the puzzle?

B	Y
C	X
E	V
G	T
K	P
M	?

Which of the lower circles replaces the question mark?

Which number replaces the question mark and completes the puzzle?

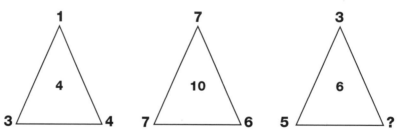

23 PUZZLE

Which letter completes the puzzle?

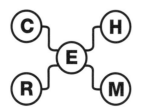
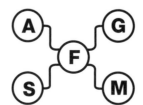
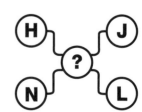

24

PUZZLE 24

What is missing from the last star?

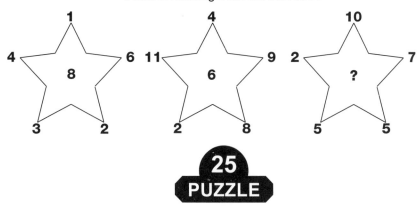

PUZZLE 25

Which letter completes the puzzle?

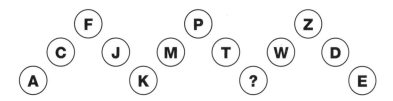

PUZZLE 26

Which number replaces the question mark and completes the puzzle?

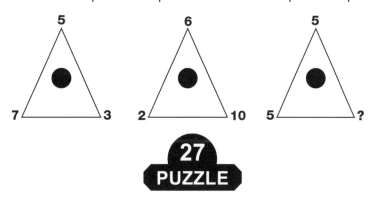

PUZZLE 27

Which number replaces the question mark and completes the puzzle?

 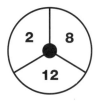 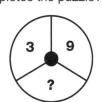

T
E
S
T

2

25

Which segment completes the puzzle?

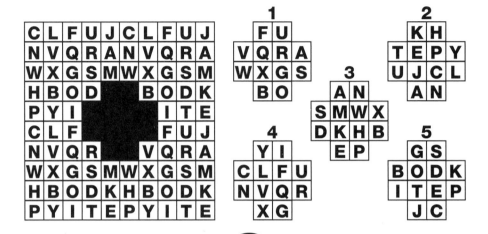

C	L	F	U	J	C	L	F	U	J
N	V	Q	R	A	N	V	Q	R	A
W	X	G	S	M	W	X	G	S	M
H	B	O	D	■	■	B	O	D	K
P	Y	I	■	■	■	■	I	T	E
C	L	F	■	■	■	■	F	U	J
N	V	Q	R	■	■	V	Q	R	A
W	X	G	S	M	W	X	G	S	M
H	B	O	D	K	H	B	O	D	K
P	Y	I	T	E	P	Y	I	T	E

1

F	U
V	Q	R	A
W	X	G	S
	B	O

2

K	H
T	E	P	Y
U	J	C	L
	A	N

3

A	N
S	M	W	X
D	K	H	B
	E	P

4

Y	I
C	L	F	U
N	V	Q	R
X	G

5

G	S
B	O	D	K
I	T	E	P
J	C

29
PUZZLE

Which letter replaces the question mark and completes the puzzle?

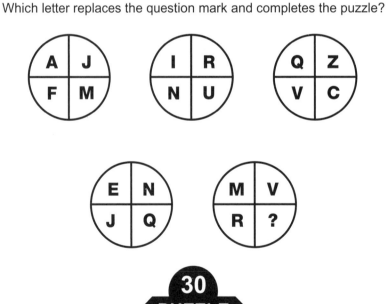

A	J
F	M

I	R
N	U

Q	Z
V	C

E	N
J	Q

M	V
R	?

30
PUZZLE

Which letter follows the sequence to complete the puzzle?

A H F M K R P ?

TEST 2

1 PUZZLE

Which number replaces the question mark and completes the sequence?

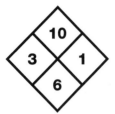
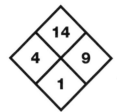

2 PUZZLE

Which number replaces the question mark and completes the sequence?

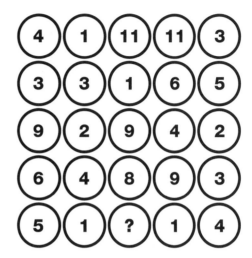

3 PUZZLE

Which number replaces the question mark and completes the sequence?

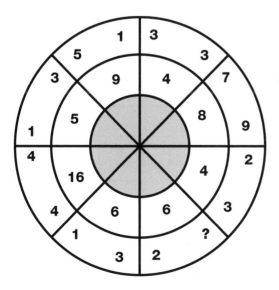

4 PUZZLE

Which letter replaces the question mark and completes the sequence?

13	INC	2
6	QRG	7
4	DOM	8
7	SUI	7
8	AD?	2

27

5 PUZZLE

Which letter replaces the question mark and completes the sequence?

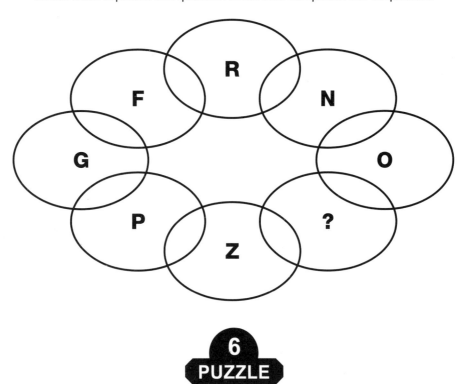

6 PUZZLE

Which number replaces the question mark and completes the sequence?

4	2	8	7
6	3	6	6
5	1	5	3

1	0	8	8
7	1	4	2
8	7	2	9

3	2	4	8
2	1	8	9
7	4	9	7

3	0	6	2
4	1	6	4
6	3	?	5

PUZZLE 7

Which letter replaces the question mark and completes the puzzle?

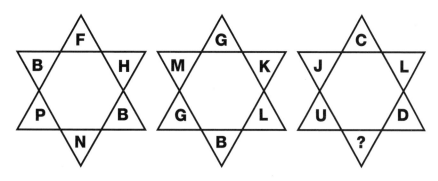

PUZZLE 8

Which number replaces the question mark and completes the puzzle?

3		9
7	2	2
4		1

1		6
5	7	3
4		8

9		8
2	1	7
6		3

4		5
8	?	1
2		3

PUZZLE 9

Which letter replaces the question mark and completes the puzzle?

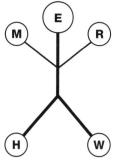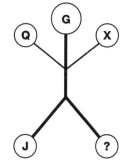

PUZZLE 10

Which letter replaces the question mark and completes the puzzle?

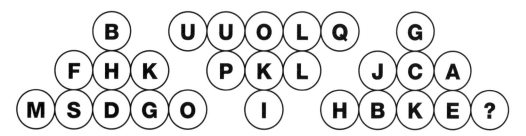

29

11 PUZZLE

Which number replaces the question mark and completes the puzzle?

1	7	9
3	6	3
5	4	2
2	7	5
2	6	?

12 PUZZLE

Which letter replaces the question mark and completes the puzzle?

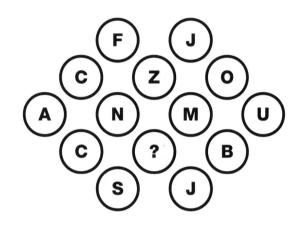

13 PUZZLE

Which number replaces the question mark and completes the puzzle?

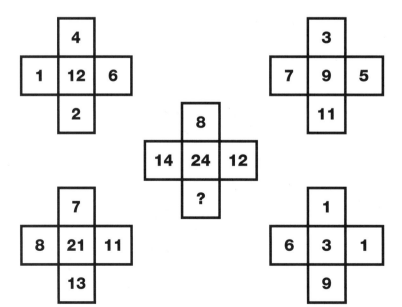

14
PUZZLE

Which letter replaces the question mark and completes the puzzle?

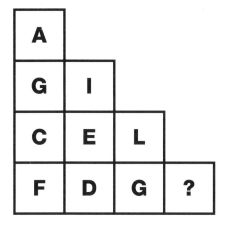

15
PUZZLE

Which number replaces the question mark and completes the puzzle?

16
PUZZLE

Which playing card replaces the question mark and completes the puzzle?

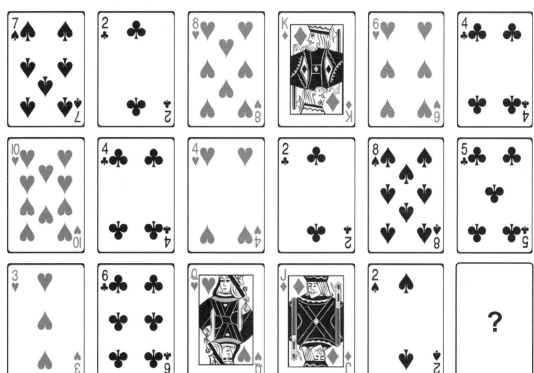

17 PUZZLE

Which letter replaces the question mark and completes the sequence?

P	U
K	P

Z	E
U	J

F	K
A	D

?	O
Y	T

18 PUZZLE

Which letter replaces the question mark and completes the puzzle?

D		F		I	
	X		R		M
E		M		O	
	A		V		R
G		N		V	
	E		A		?

19 PUZZLE

Where should the missing hour hand point?

20 PUZZLE

Which letter replaces the question mark and completes the puzzle?

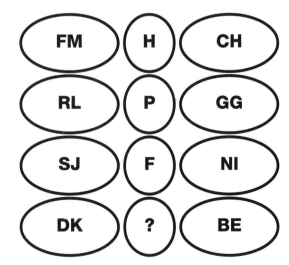

FM   H   CH

RL   P   GG

SJ   F   NI

DK   ?   BE

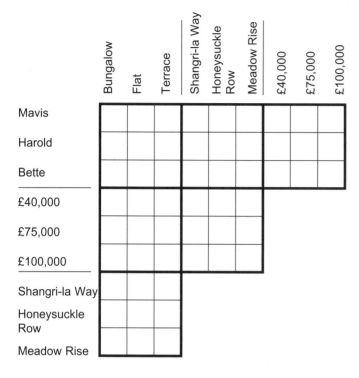

	Bungalow	Flat	Terrace	Shangri-la Way	Honeysuckle Row	Meadow Rise	£40,000	£75,000	£100,000
Mavis									
Harold									
Bette									
£40,000									
£75,000									
£100,000									
Shangri-la Way									
Honeysuckle Row									
Meadow Rise									

Mavis, Harold and Bette all own properties in rather exclusive areas of the town, and have recently had them valued. Harold lives in Meadow Rise, but his property is not worth £75,000. The property in Honeysuckle Row worked out as the cheapest, despite it being a lovely road. Bette lives in a terrace house, although there are no terraced houses along Shangri-La Way. Mavis's property is not a bungalow. Can you deduce from these clues which person lives where, in which property, and how much the property was valued.

Owner	Property	Road	Value

Which letter replaces the question mark and completes the puzzle?

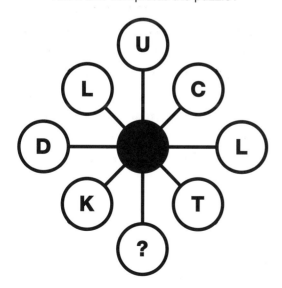

Which number replaces the question mark and completes the puzzle?

6	EJI	3
M F K		D P G
9	NRG	?

TEST

3

24 PUZZLE

Which picture cube does this shape make?

A

C

B

D

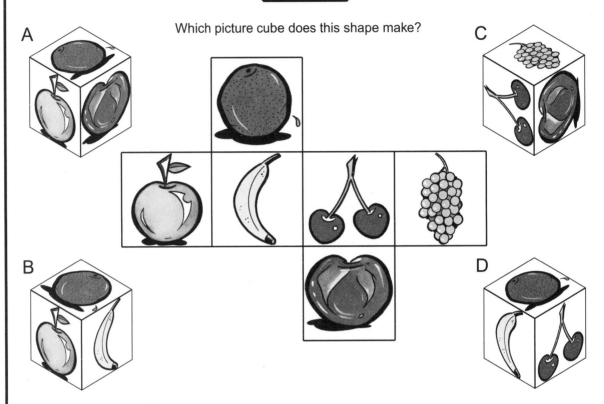

25 PUZZLE

Which letter replaces the question mark and completes the puzzle?

D	G	D
	H	L
	Y	
	R	L
S	K	?

26 PUZZLE

Joe and John are playing marbles. If Joe loses one marble to John, they will both have the same number of marbles, but if John loses one marble to Joe, Joe will have twice the number of marbles as John. How many marbles do the two boys currently have?

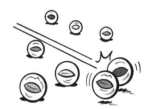

27 PUZZLE

Which number replaces the question mark and completes the puzzle?

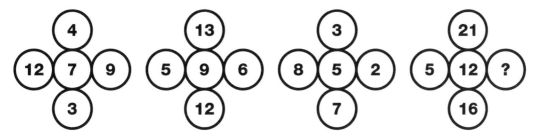

28 PUZZLE

Which number replaces the question mark and completes the puzzle?

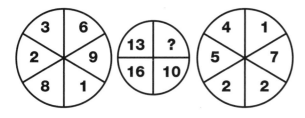

29 PUZZLE

Which number replaces the question mark and completes the puzzle?

3	12	6
	15	
	18	

2	7	5
	9	
	12	

11	4	8
	15	
	12	

8	3	4
	11	
	?	

30 PUZZLE

Which domino replaces the question mark to complete the puzzle?

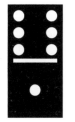 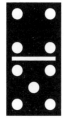    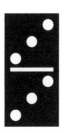 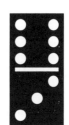 

PUZZLE 1

Which number is missing?

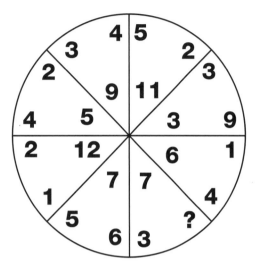

PUZZLE 2

Which letter completes the puzzle?

F	K	L	Q
A	K	Z	V
M	I	H	D
H	C	N	?

PUZZLE 3

Which symbol replaces the question mark and completes the puzzle?

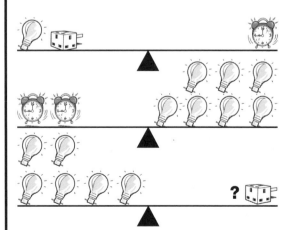

PUZZLE 4

Which number replaces the question mark and completes the puzzle?

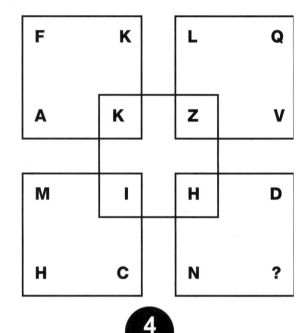

PUZZLE 5

What is missing from the last circle?

PUZZLE 6

Which letter replaces the question mark and completes the puzzle?

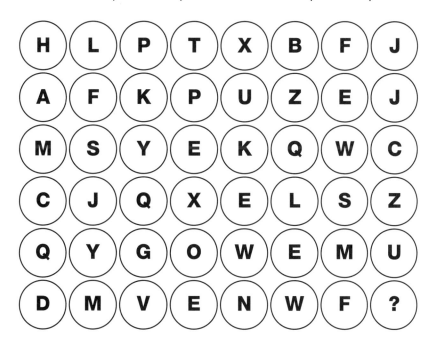

PUZZLE 7

What is missing from the bottom left circle?

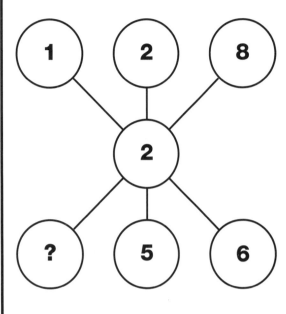

PUZZLE 8

Which letter completes the puzzle?

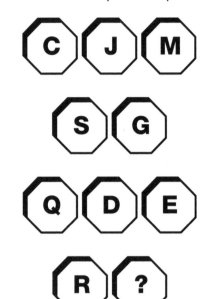

PUZZLE 9

Which number replaces the question mark and completes the puzzle?

32	45	60	77	?

PUZZLE 10

Which number replaces the question mark and completes the puzzle?

3	5
4	1
4	7
5	3
5	?

11 PUZZLE

What is missing from the last circle?

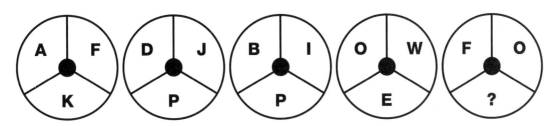

12 PUZZLE

Which number replaces the question mark and completes the puzzle?

13 PUZZLE

Which letter completes the puzzle?

14 PUZZLE

Which number replaces the question mark and completes the puzzle?

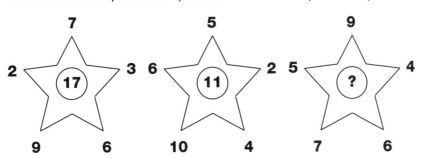

39

PUZZLE 15

What is missing from the last circle?

 H C Z

 K F W

N Q ?

PUZZLE 16

Which number completes the puzzle?

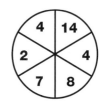

4 | 14
2 | 4
7 | 8

6 | 6
1 | 2
3 | 12

5 | 12
2 | 4
? | 10

PUZZLE 17

Which of the bottom letters replaces the question mark and completes the puzzle?

L	Z	E
T	A	M
V	N	?

H D X W B

TEST

4

40

What is missing from the last oval?

7122

6521

8332

4743

9911

387?

Which number completes the puzzle?

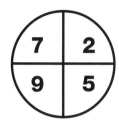

Which letter replaces the question mark and completes the puzzle?

B	H

C	E

D	B

D	I

E	F

F	?

4

21 PUZZLE

What is missing from the central circle?

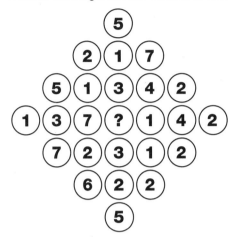

22 PUZZLE

Which single digit number replaces the question mark?

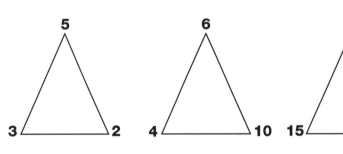

23 PUZZLE

Which letter completes the puzzle?

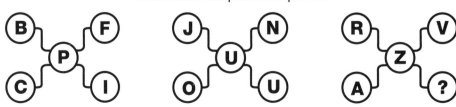

42

PUZZLE 24

What is missing from the last star?

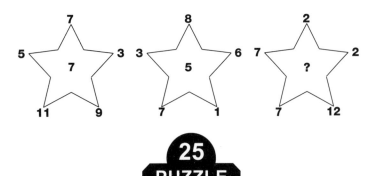

PUZZLE 25

Which letter completes the puzzle?

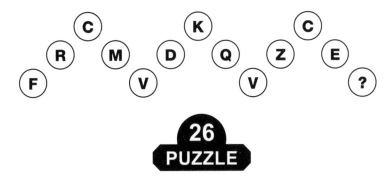

PUZZLE 26

Which number replaces the question mark and completes the puzzle?

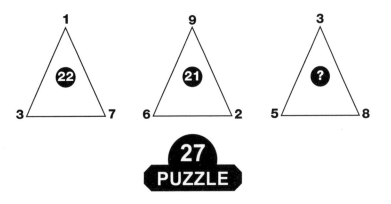

PUZZLE 27

Which letter replaces the question mark and completes the puzzle?

Which shape completes the puzzle?

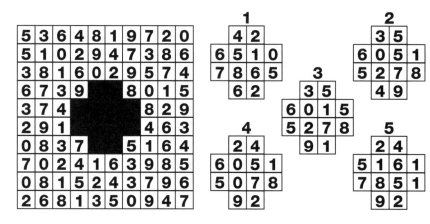

5	3	6	4	8	1	9	7	2	0
5	1	0	2	9	4	7	3	8	6
3	8	1	6	0	2	9	5	7	4
6	7	3	9	■	■	8	0	1	5
3	7	4	■	■	■	8	2	9	
2	9	1	■	■	■	4	6	3	
0	8	3	7	■	5	1	6	4	
7	0	2	4	1	6	3	9	8	5
0	8	1	5	2	4	3	7	9	6
2	6	8	1	3	5	0	9	4	7

1

4	2		
6	5	1	0
7	8	6	5
6	2		

2

3	5		
6	0	5	1
5	2	7	8
4	9		

3

3	5		
6	0	1	5
5	2	7	8
9	1		

4

2	4		
6	0	5	1
5	0	7	8
9	2		

5

2	4		
5	1	6	1
7	8	5	1
9	2		

Which number replaces the question mark and completes the puzzle?

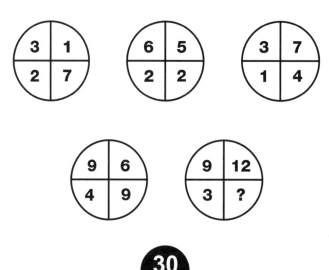

Which letter replaces the question mark and completes the puzzle?

B C E G K M Q ?

PUZZLE 1

Which grid replaces the question mark?

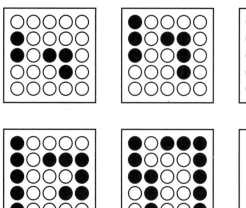

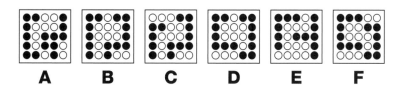

A   B   C   D   E   F

PUZZLE 2

Which time from the choices given follows the sequence?

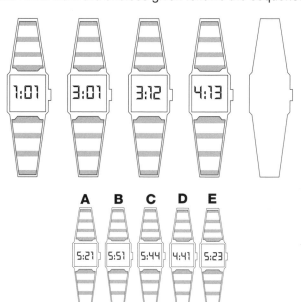

A   B   C   D   E

5

PUZZLE 3

Which letter replaces the question mark from the choices given below?

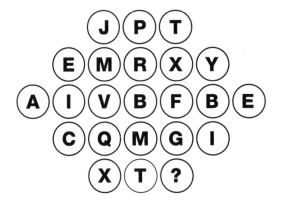

PUZZLE 4

Which number replaces the question mark and completes the puzzle?

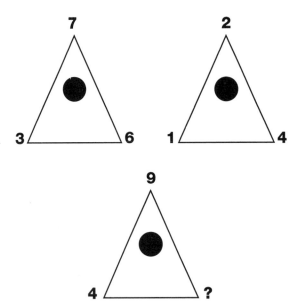

PUZZLE 5

What is missing from this wheel?

PUZZLE 6

Which letter completes the puzzle?

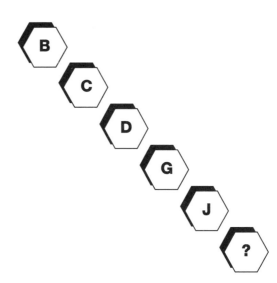

PUZZLE 7

Which number replaces the question mark and completes the puzzle?

72

69

64

57

48

?

PUZZLE 8

Which number replaces the question mark and completes the puzzle?

9 PUZZLE

What is missing from the last hexagon?

10 PUZZLE

Which letter completes the puzzle?

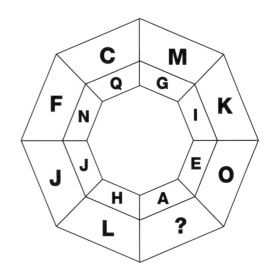

11 PUZZLE

Which number replaces the question mark and completes the puzzle?

12 PUZZLE

Which number replaces the question mark and completes the puzzle?

2	7	3	6
4	1	4	5
6	8	8	1
1	4	0	?

13 PUZZLE

What is missing from the last hexagon?

14 PUZZLE

Which letter completes the puzzle?

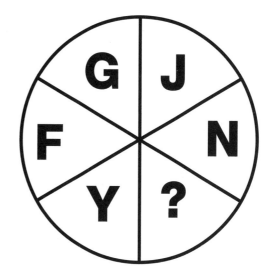

15 PUZZLE

Which number replaces the question
mark and completes the puzzle?

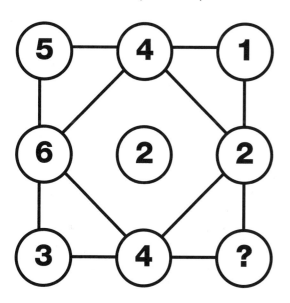

16 PUZZLE

Where should the hour hand be
pointing on the bottom clock?

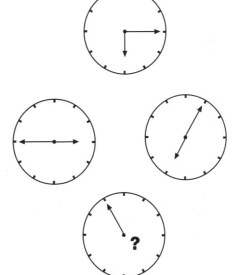

PUZZLE 17

What is missing from the last shape?

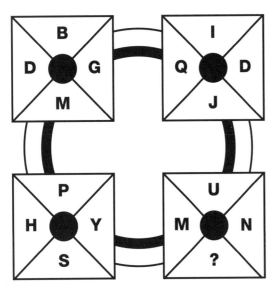

PUZZLE 17

What is missing from the last shape?

| 1 | 5 | 9 | 15 | ? |

PUZZLE 18

Which letter completes the puzzle?

A

E

F

H

?

PUZZLE 19

Which letter replaces the question mark and completes the puzzle?

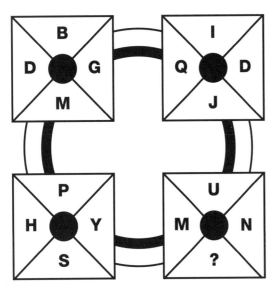

B
D G
M

I
Q D
J

P
H Y
S

U
M N
?

PUZZLE 20

Which number replaces the question mark and completes the chain?

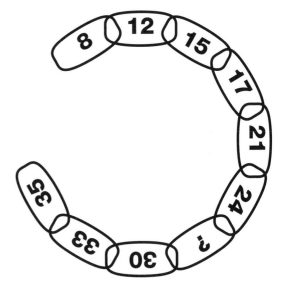

8 12 15 17 21 24 ? 30 33 35

PUZZLE 21

What is missing from the last circle?

2 4 6

10

16 26 ?

PUZZLE 22

Which letter completes the puzzle?

X ?

R P J

L F

PUZZLE 23

Which number replaces the question mark and completes the puzzle?

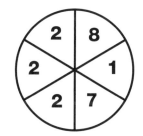 

8	10
14	9
2	11

2	8
2	1
2	7

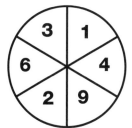 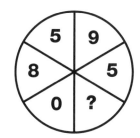

3	1
6	4
2	9

5	9
8	5
0	?

PUZZLE 24

Which number replaces the question mark and completes the puzzle?

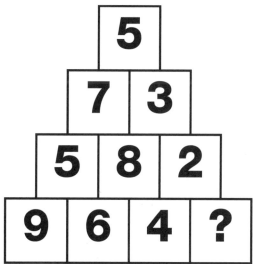

5

7 3

5 8 2

9 6 4 ?

T
E
S
T

5

25 PUZZLE

What is missing from the last circle?

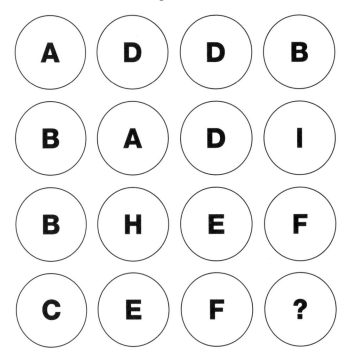

A	D	D	B
B	A	D	I
B	H	E	F
C	E	F	?

26 PUZZLE

Which number replaces the question mark and completes the puzzle?

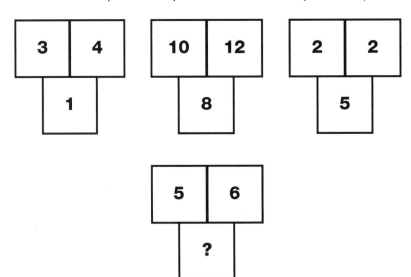

| 3 | 4 |
| 1 | |

| 10 | 12 |
| 8 | |

| 2 | 2 |
| 5 | |

| 5 | 6 |
| ? | |

PUZZLE 27

What is missing from the last square?

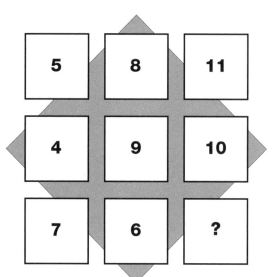

PUZZLE 28

Which letter completes the puzzle?

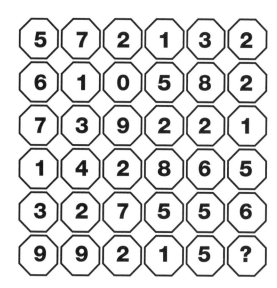

PUZZLE 29

Which number is the odd one out in each oval?

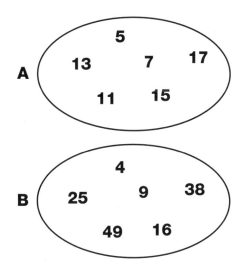

A: 5, 13, 7, 17, 11, 15

B: 4, 25, 9, 38, 49, 16

PUZZLE 30

Which number replaces the question mark and completes the puzzle?

5   **4**   7

12   **6**   6

7   **?**   2

T
E
S
T

5

53

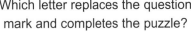

PUZZLE 1

Which letter replaces the question mark and completes the puzzle?

PUZZLE 2

Which letter replaces the question mark and completes the puzzle?

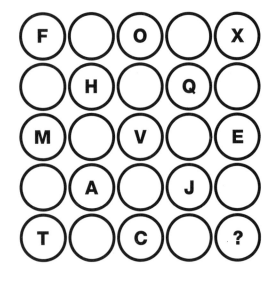

PUZZLE 3

Which number is missing?

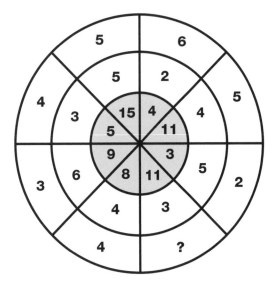

PUZZLE 4

Which letter replaces the question mark and completes the puzzle?

E	LRCEX	C
I	IPHTL	D
M	XFTMH	B
N	RLXNF	C
?	OYJTQ	E

PUZZLE 5

Which letter completes this chain?

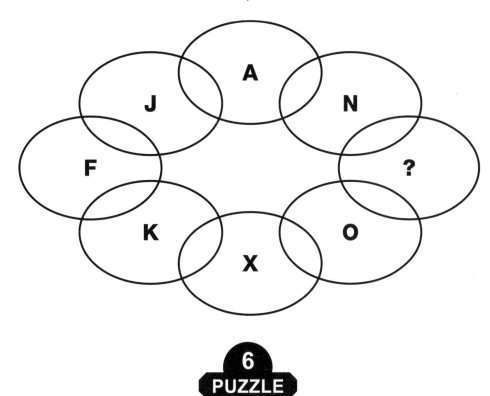

PUZZLE 6

Which number replaces the question mark and completes the puzzle?

3	6	2	6
2	7	5	15
11	5	10	1

9	1	17	3
2	3	6	1
9	2	4	0

12	7	19	9
4	10	11	16
20	7	14	1

6	5	15	3
0	4	1	14
2	3	6	?

7 PUZZLE

Which letter replaces the question mark in the last star?

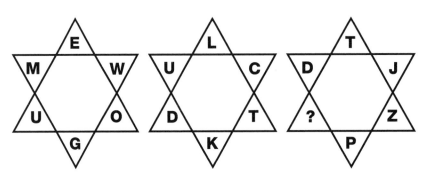

8 PUZZLE

Which number completes the puzzle?

6		1
L	P	D
2		4

5		1
J	M	C
2		3

4		4
L	T	H
3		2

3		2
O	U	F
5		?

9 PUZZLE

Which number replaces the question mark and completes the puzzle?

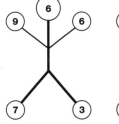
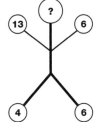

10 PUZZLE

Which letter replaces the question mark and completes the puzzle?

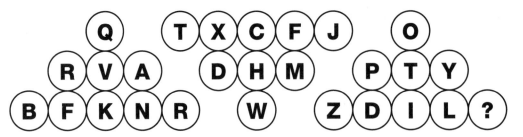

PUZZLE 11

Which letter replaces the question mark?

3	P	8
9	G	11
2	U	4
3	W	1
7	?	18

PUZZLE 12

Which number is missing from the puzzle?

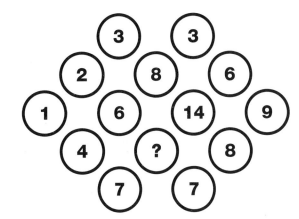

PUZZLE 13

Which number do you need to add to complete the puzzle?

	6	
5	23	2
	4	

	3	
3	17	15
	4	

	8	
6	14	8
	1	

	7	
2	25	?
	4	

6

6

14 PUZZLE

Which letter is missing?

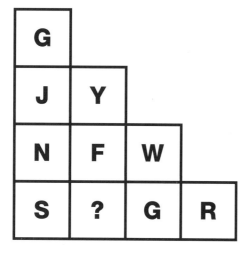

15 PUZZLE

Which letter replaces the question mark and completes the puzzle?

A	H
V	Q

Z	E
U	L

Q	X
L	G

T	C
M	H

Y	D
P	?

16 PUZZLE

Which playing card replaces the question mark and completes the puzzle?

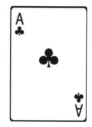

PUZZLE 17

Which letter completes this puzzle?

D	L
A	C

M	F
A	E

L	H
D	K

Q	I
B	?

PUZZLE 18

Which number will complete the grid?

1	0	0	2	5	6
1	2	1	2	8	9
1	4	4	3	2	4
1	6	9	3	6	1
1	9	6	4	0	0
2	2	5	4	4	?

PUZZLE 19

What time should the bottom clock show?

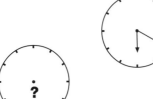

PUZZLE 20

Which letter replaces the question mark and completes the puzzle?

CB	13	AI
FE	26	IA
DH	25	BC
EB	35	H?

21 PUZZLE

	Coventry Amateur Dramatics	Real Shakespeare Co.	Piecrust Players	March	June	October	£3	£6	£10
Julius Caesar									
Othello									
Macbeth									
£3									
£6									
£10									
March									
June									
October									

Newtown has always had a thriving amateur dramatics scene. This year, the Piecrust Players were putting on a production of Macbeth. Othello, which was not performed by the Coventry Amateur Dramatics, had the cheapest tickets. Julius Caesar was the production put on in March and, although it had the best set yet seen in Newtown, was not the most expensive to see. The Real Shakespeare Company's production was put on later than the Piecrust Players' one. From this information, can you work out which group put on which play, the cost of the tickets and the month in which the plays could be seen?

Theatre group	Play	Opening month	Ticket price

22 PUZZLE

Which number is missing from this puzzle?

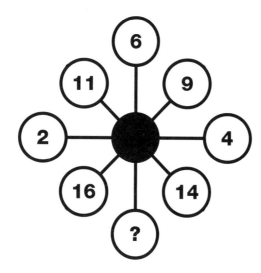

23 PUZZLE

Which letter replaces the question mark and completes the sequence?

J	O?J	V
L O S		I W L
X	DKS	B

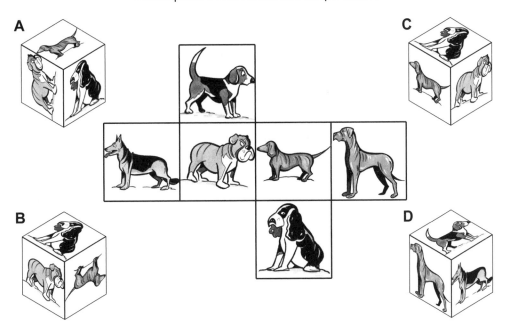

PUZZLE 24

Which picture cube does this shape make?

A

C

B

D

PUZZLE 25

Which number replaces the question mark and completes the puzzle?

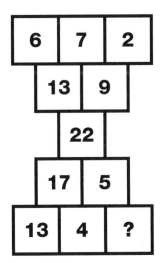

6	7	2
13	9	
22		
17	5	
13	4	?

PUZZLE 26

Penelope buys a small bottle of her favourite perfume for £10. If the perfume is worth £9 more than the cost of the ornate bottle it comes in, how much is the bottle worth?

Which letter is missing from the last grid?

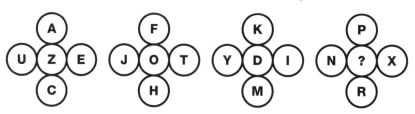

- Grid 1: A / U Z E / C
- Grid 2: F / J O T / H
- Grid 3: K / Y D I / M
- Grid 4: P / N ? X / R

Which letter is missing from the puzzle?

- Circle 1: H L / B P / X T
- Circle 2: F R / J N
- Circle 3: V Z / P D / L ?

Which letter replaces the question mark and completes the puzzle?

J	O	T
	U	
	A	

D	J	P
	Q	
	X	

M	T	A
	B	
	J	

V	D	L
	M	
	?	

What is required to complete the puzzle?

PUZZLE 1

What is missing from the last grid?

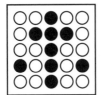 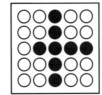 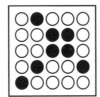

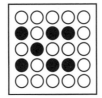 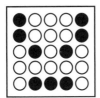

A   **B**   **C**   **D**   **E**   **F**

PUZZLE 2

Which watch shown below fills the missing space?

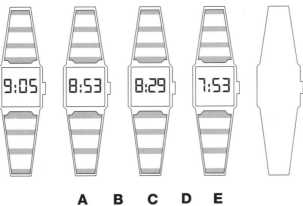

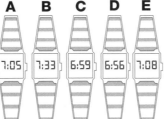

A   **B**   **C**   **D**   **E**

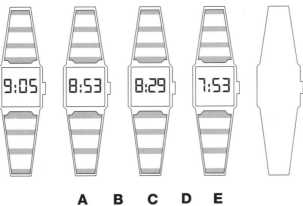

3 PUZZLE

What is missing from the last circle?

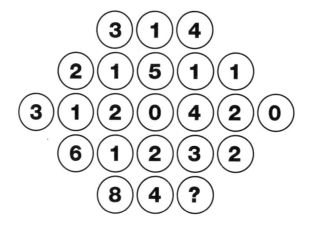

4 PUZZLE

Which number replaces the question mark and completes the puzzle?

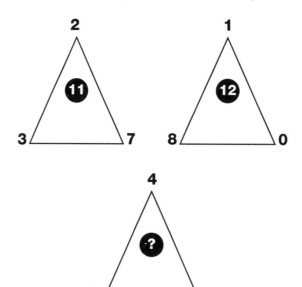

What is missing from the last segment?

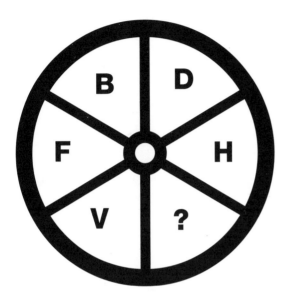

Which number completes the puzzle?

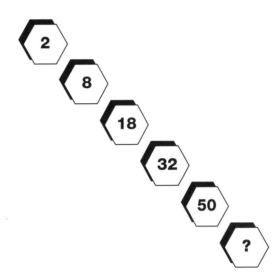

7 PUZZLE

Which number replaces the question mark and completes the puzzle?

6

8

12

20

36

?

8 PUZZLE

Which number replaces the question mark to complete the triangle?

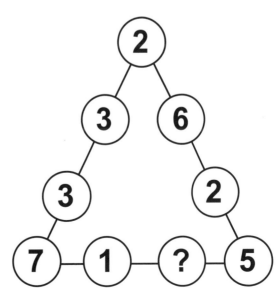

9 PUZZLE

What is missing from the last hexagon?

B   B   E

B   E   F

B   H   ?

10 PUZZLE

Which letter completes the puzzle?

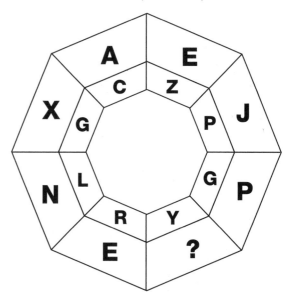

A   E
C   Z
X   J
G   P
N   G   P
L   Y
R
E   ?

11 PUZZLE

Which number replaces the question mark and completes the puzzle?

5
8
10
11
14
?

12 PUZZLE

Which number replaces the question mark and completes the puzzle?

7	3	2	6
9	2	4	3
1	5	7	5
0	6	5	?

PUZZLE 13

What is missing from the last hexagon?

PUZZLE 14

Which letter completes the puzzle?

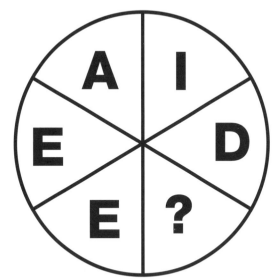

PUZZLE 15

Which number replaces the question mark and completes the puzzle?

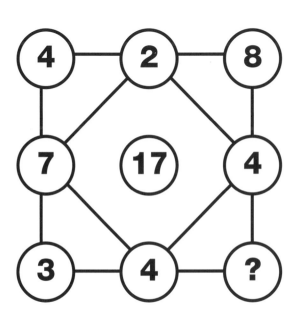

PUZZLE 16

Where should the hour hand point to on the bottom clock?

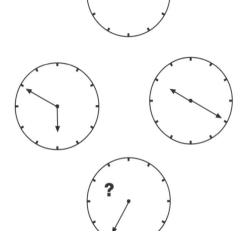

PUZZLE 17

What is missing from the last hexagon?

B F J P ?

PUZZLE 18

Which letter completes the puzzle?

A

B

D

F

?

PUZZLE 19

Which number replaces the question mark and completes the puzzle?

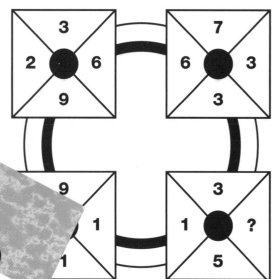

PUZZLE 20

Which number replaces the question mark and completes the chain?

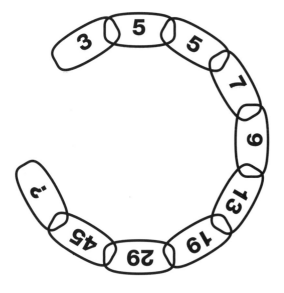

21 PUZZLE

What is missing from the last circle?

22 PUZZLE

Which number completes the puzzle?

23 PUZZLE

Which number replaces the question mark and completes the puzzle?

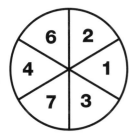 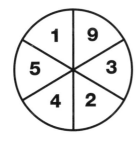

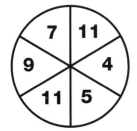 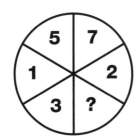

24 PUZZLE

Which letter replaces the question mark and completes the puzzle?

T E S T 7

69

PUZZLE 25

What is missing from the last circle?

E	L	B	I
G	D	F	M
J	A	F	B
C	H	K	?

PUZZLE 26

Which letter replaces the question mark and completes the puzzle?

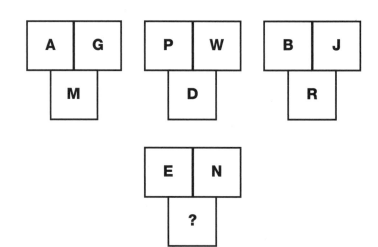

What is missing from the last square?

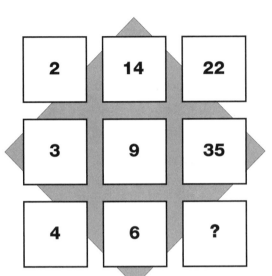

Which number completes the puzzle?

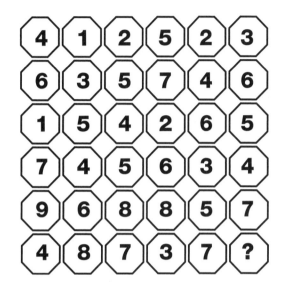

Which two numbers are the odd ones out in each of these ovals?

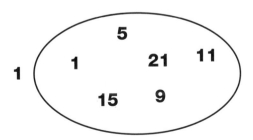

Which number replaces the question mark and completes the puzzle?

TEST

7

PUZZLE 1

What is missing from the last segment?

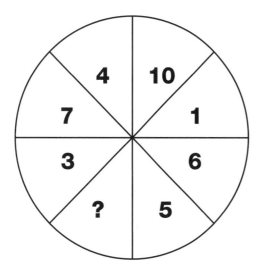

PUZZLE 2

Which letter completes the puzzle?

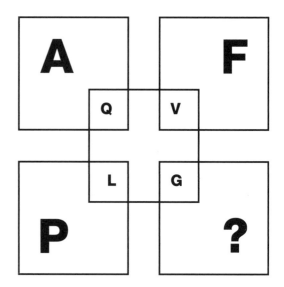

PUZZLE 3

What object is needed to make
the scales balance?

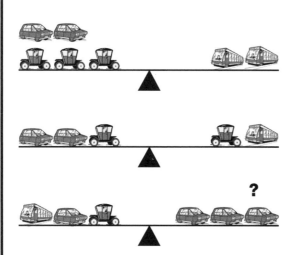

PUZZLE 4
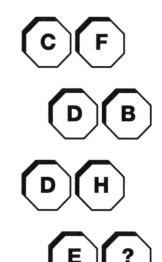

Which letter replaces the question
mark and completes the puzzle?

PUZZLE 5

What is missing from the last circle?

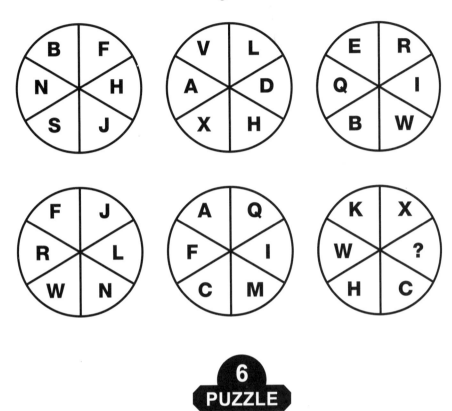

PUZZLE 6

Which letter replaces the question mark and completes the puzzle?

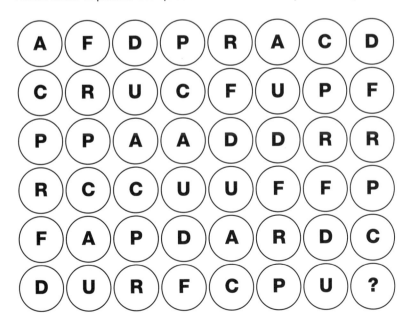

PUZZLE 7

What is missing from the last circle?

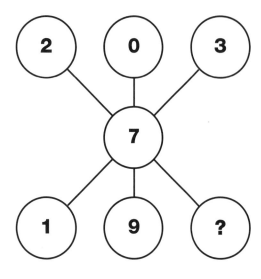

PUZZLE 8

Which letter completes the puzzle?

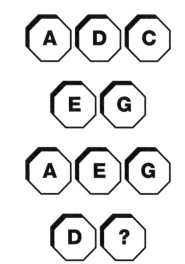

PUZZLE 9

Which number replaces the question mark and completes the puzzle?

PUZZLE 10

Which number replaces the question mark and completes the puzzle?

2	3
6	4
8	12
24	?

11 PUZZLE

What is missing from the middle circle?

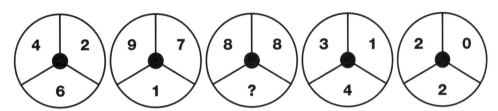

12 PUZZLE

Which number replaces the question mark and completes the puzzle?

3	1	7
7	5	11
12	10	?

13 PUZZLE

Which letter completes the puzzle?

14 PUZZLE

Which number replaces the question mark and completes the puzzle?

8

What is missing from the last circle?

(A) (G) (H)

(D) (L) (P)

(N) (F) (?)

Which letter completes the puzzle?

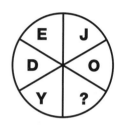

Which number replaces the question mark and completes the puzzle?

3	12	7
4	15	9
6	11	?

18 PUZZLE

What is missing from the last oval?

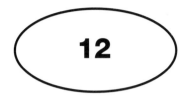

12

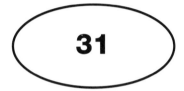

31

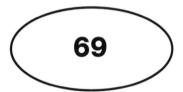

69

145

297

?

19 PUZZLE

Which letter completes the puzzle?

E	K
P	F

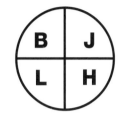

B	J
L	H

D	M
Q	I

C	O
R	?

20 PUZZLE

Which number replaces the question mark and completes the puzzle?

3	4

4	5

6	8

11	16

24	37

58	?

21 PUZZLE

Which of the letters below is missing from the bottom circle?

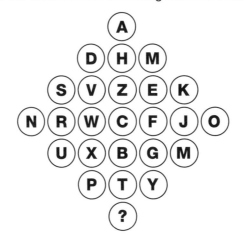

22 PUZZLE

Which number replaces the question mark and completes the puzzle?

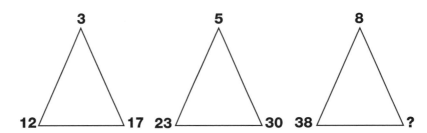

23 PUZZLE

Which letter completes the puzzle?

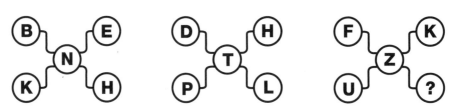

PUZZLE 24

What is missing from the last star?

  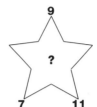

PUZZLE 25

Which letter completes the puzzle?

PUZZLE 26

Which number replaces the question mark and completes the puzzle?

PUZZLE 27

Which number replaces the question mark and completes the puzzle?

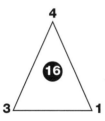 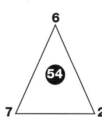 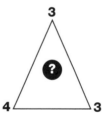

Which segment fills the gap?

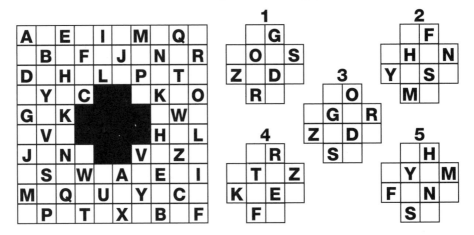

Which number replaces the question mark and completes the puzzle?

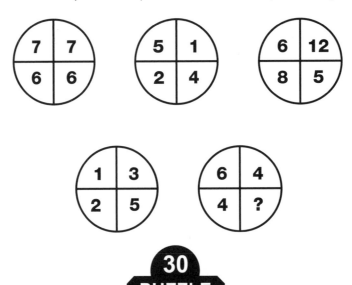

Which number replaces the question mark and completes the sequence?

PUZZLE 1

Which letter replaces the question mark and completes the sequence?

PUZZLE 2

Which single-digit number replaces the question mark and completes the puzzle?

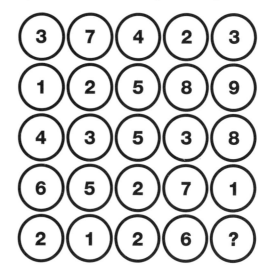

PUZZLE 3

Which number replaces the question mark and completes the puzzle?

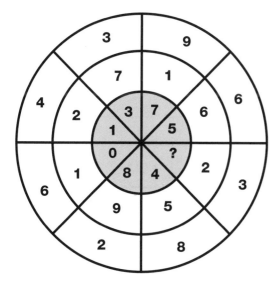

PUZZLE 4

Which letter is missing?

A	DH	M
F	KN	R
L	PU	X
S	VZ	E
X	CF	?

PUZZLE 5

Which number replaces the question mark and completes the sequence?

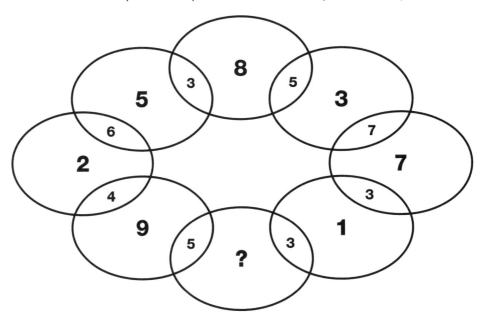

Numbers: 8, 3, 5, 5, 3, 6, 2, 7, 7, 4, 3, 9, 5, ?, 3, 1

PUZZLE 6

Which number completes the bottom grid?

3	5	4	8
1	11	7	3
2	6	1	12

4	7	8	13
5	14	9	11
9	7	4	13

1	2	4	5
4	3	2	8
7	1	3	1

2	3	0	3
3	8	5	5
5	5	2	?

Which letter replaces the question mark and completes the puzzle?

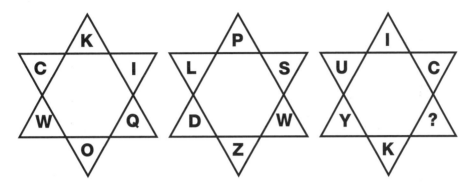

Which number replaces the question mark and completes the puzzle?

3		9
1	11	8
4		2

4		2
6	11	1
7		3

2		6
8	2	4
3		5

4		1
2	?	3
6		2

Which number completes the puzzle?

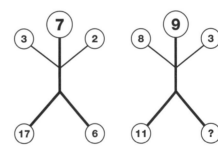

Which number replaces the question mark on the third triangle?

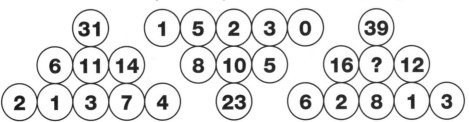

11 PUZZLE

Which number replaces the question mark to complete the puzzle?

3	5	3
2	4	7
8	4	3
6	2	9
2	11	?

12 PUZZLE

Which number replaces the question mark and completes the sequence?

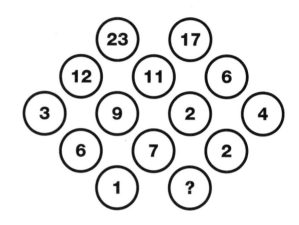

23 17

12 11 6

3 9 2 4

6 7 2

1 ?

13 PUZZLE

Which letter replaces the question mark and completes the puzzle?

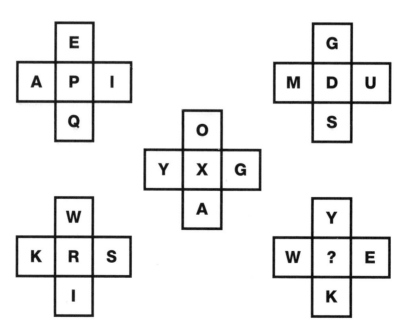

E
A P I
Q

G
M D U
S

O
Y X G
A

W
K R S
I

Y
W ? E
K

14 PUZZLE

Which number replaces the question mark and completes the puzzle?

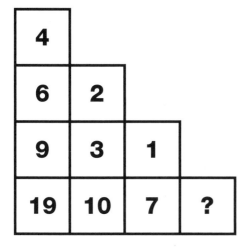

4			
6	2		
9	3	1	
19	10	7	?

15 PUZZLE

Which number replaces the question mark to finish this puzzle?

2	1
7	5

3	4
2	2

5	5
9	7

10	5
63	35

15	20
18	?

16 PUZZLE

Which playing card replaces the question mark and completes the puzzle?

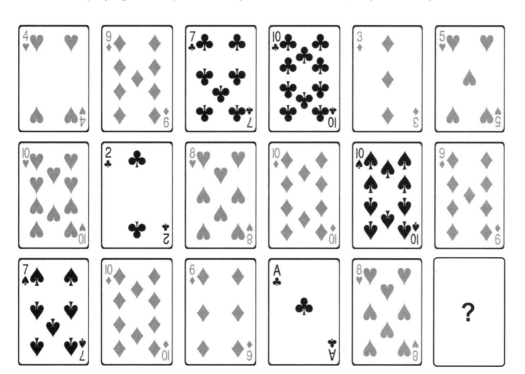

PUZZLE 17

Which letter replaces the question mark and completes the sequence?

A	M
J	U

R	F
B	S

E	P
P	H

I	Z
Y	?

PUZZLE 18

Which letter replaces the question mark and completes the grid?

B		N		Z	
	H		T		F
Q		E		S	
	X		L		Z
E		U		K	
	M		C		?

PUZZLE 19

Where should the missing hour hand point to?

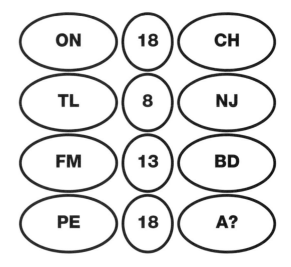

PUZZLE 20

Which letter completes this puzzle?

ON	18	CH
TL	8	NJ
FM	13	BD
PE	18	A?

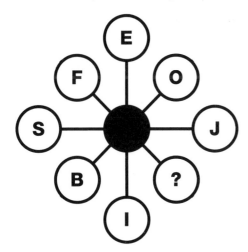

21 PUZZLE

	Bob	Mike	Sandra	Monday	Wednesday	Friday	Roses	Potatoes	Apples
Housemaid's knee									
Tennis elbow									
Bad back									
Roses									
Potatoes									
Apples									
Monday									
Wednesday									
Friday									

Bob, Mike and Sandra are all keen gardeners, and are proud of their allotments. Without the knee problems that affect some of his friends, Bob produces the best roses in the village. Sandra, who suffers from tennis elbow, only gets the chance to work on Mondays. The person who grows apples always works on the allotments on a Friday.

There is enough information above to work out what kind of injury each gardener tends to suffer from, who produces which crop, and on which day of the week each can usually be found at the allotments.

Gardener	Injury	Crop	Day

22 PUZZLE

Which letter replaces the question mark and completes the sequence?

E, F, O, S, J, B, ?, I

23 PUZZLE

Which letter replaces the question mark and completes the sequence?

U		K		B
	O		S	
E				F
	C		C	
M		R		?

24 PUZZLE

Which picture cube does this shape make?

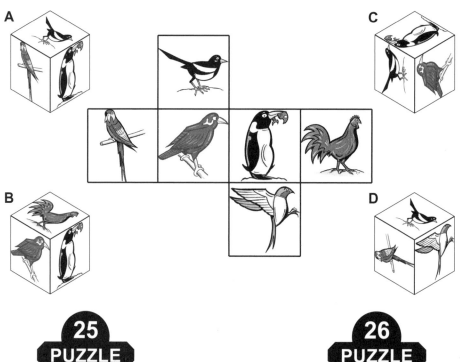

A

B

C

D

25 PUZZLE

Which letter replaces the question mark and completes the puzzle?

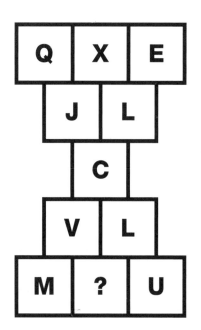

| Q | X | E |
| J | L |
| C |
| V | L |
| M | ? | U |

26 PUZZLE

For Christmas this year, the Taylor family had a get together. The following people were present: one grandmother, one grandfather, two mothers, two fathers, one father-in-law, one mother-in-law, one daughter-in-law, four children, three grandchildren, one brother, two sisters, two sons and two daughters. What is the fewest number of individuals that could have been there?

PUZZLE 27

Which letter replaces the question mark and completes the puzzle?

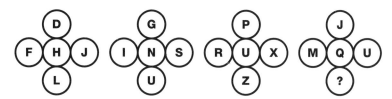

Circle 1: D / F H J / L
Circle 2: G / I N S / U
Circle 3: P / R U X / Z
Circle 4: J / M Q U / ?

PUZZLE 28

Which number replaces the question mark and completes the wheel?

Wheel 1: 4 2 3 9 6 8
Wheel 2: M I S W
Wheel 3: 6 11 2 8 1 ?

PUZZLE 29

Which letter replaces the question mark and completes the puzzle?

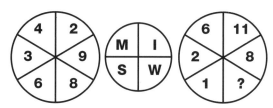

J	O	T
	Y	
	D	

N	T	Z
	F	
	L	

H	O	V
	C	
	J	

C	K	S
	A	
	?	

PUZZLE 30

What number should the last domino show on the top to complete this puzzle?

TEST

9

89

PUZZLE 1

What is missing from this wheel?

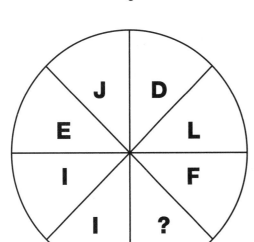

PUZZLE 2

Which number completes the puzzle?

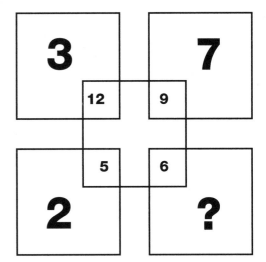

PUZZLE 3

Which symbol is needed to balance the bottom scale?

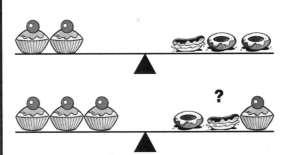

PUZZLE 4

Which letter replaces the question mark and completes the puzzle?

5
PUZZLE

What is missing from the bottom middle circle?

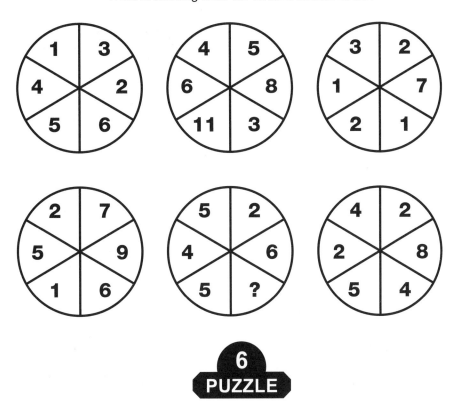

6
PUZZLE

Which letter replaces the question mark and completes the puzzle?

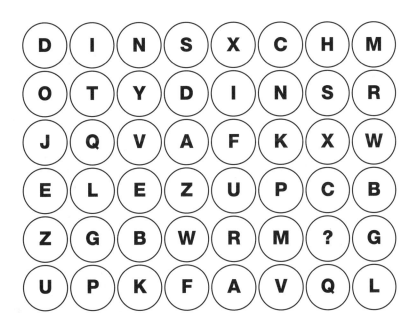

PUZZLE 7

What is missing from the bottom right hand circle?

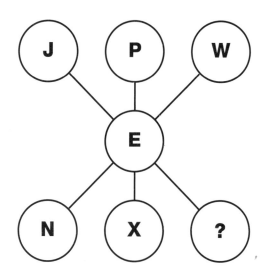

PUZZLE 8

Which number completes the puzzle?

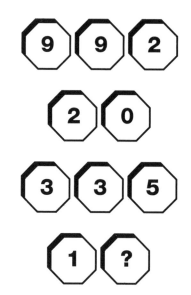

PUZZLE 9

Which number replaces the question mark and completes the puzzle?

| 26 | 22 | 18 | 12 | ? |

PUZZLE 10

Which number replaces the question mark and completes the puzzle?

2	1
3	1
4	6
6	?
9	1

11 PUZZLE

What is missing from the last circle?

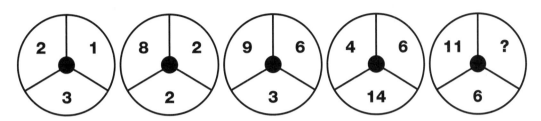

12 PUZZLE

Which number replaces the question mark and completes the puzzle?

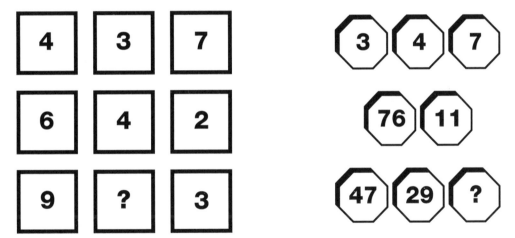

13 PUZZLE

Which number completes the puzzle?

14 PUZZLE

Which number replaces the question mark and completes the puzzle?

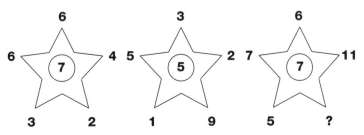

TEST

15
PUZZLE

What is missing from the last circle?

A Z E

F U J

K P ?

16
PUZZLE

Which letter completes the puzzle?

17
PUZZLE

Which of the letters below complete the puzzle?

A	E	F
H	I	K
L	M	?

N O P Q R

What is missing from the bottom oval?

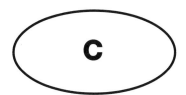

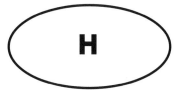

Which number completes the puzzle?

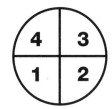

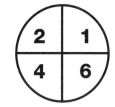

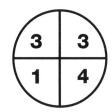

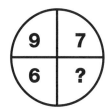

Which number replaces the question mark and completes the puzzle?

1	2

1	5

2	1

2	4

3	0

3	?

T E S T

10

21 PUZZLE

Which of the lower letters replaces the question mark to complete the puzzle?

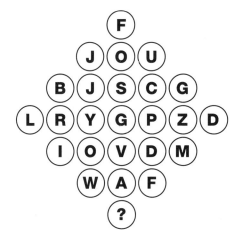

(A)(D)(H)(L)(P)(S)(V)(Z)

22 PUZZLE

Which number replaces the question mark and completes the puzzle?

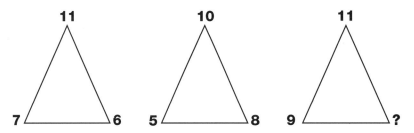

23 PUZZLE

Which number completes the puzzle?

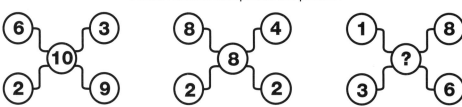

PUZZLE 24

What is missing from the last star?

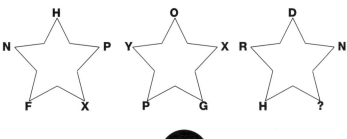

PUZZLE 25

Which letter completes the puzzle?

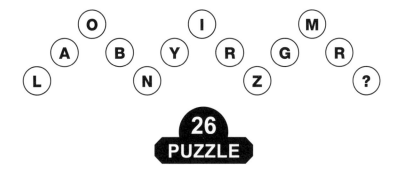

PUZZLE 26

Which number replaces the question mark and completes the puzzle?

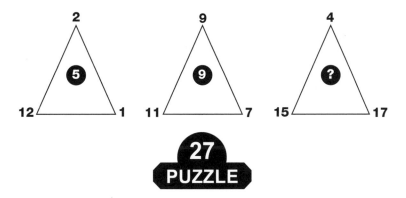

PUZZLE 27

Which number replaces the question mark and completes the puzzle?

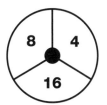

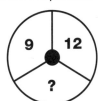

Which segment completes the puzzle?

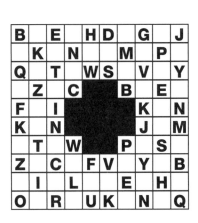

Which number replaces the question mark and completes the puzzle?

Which number replaces the question mark and completes the puzzle?

TEST
10

1 PUZZLE

What is missing from the last circle?

A   **B**   **C**   **D**   **E**   **F**

2 PUZZLE

Which watch shown below fills in the missing shape?

A   **B**   **C**   **D**   **E**

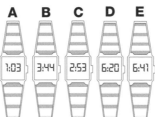

PUZZLE 3

Which of the lower circles replaces the question mark to complete the puzzle?

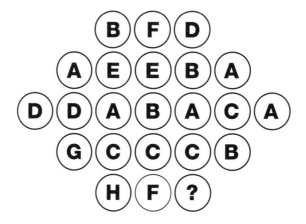

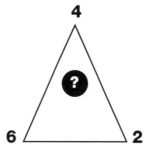

PUZZLE 4

Which number replaces the question mark and completes the puzzle?

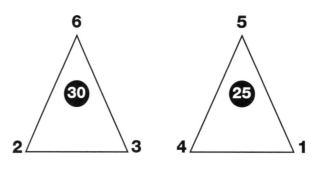

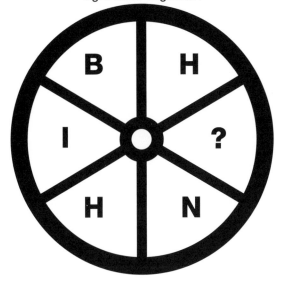

5 PUZZLE

Which letter is missing from the right-hand segment?

6 PUZZLE

Which letter completes the puzzle?

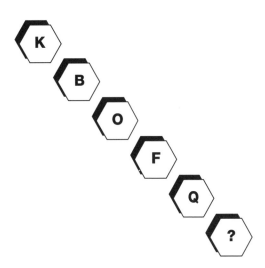

7 PUZZLE

Which number replaces the question mark and completes the puzzle?

| 36 |
| 39 |
| 44 |
| 51 |
| 60 |
| ? |

8 PUZZLE

Which letter replaces the question mark and completes the puzzle?

TEST

11

101

PUZZLE 9

What is missing from the last hexagon?

PUZZLE 10

Which letter completes the puzzle?

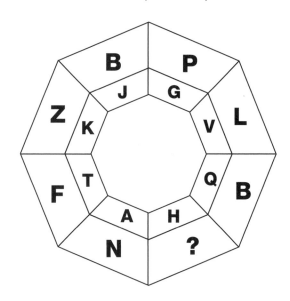

PUZZLE 11

Which number replaces the question mark and completes the puzzle?

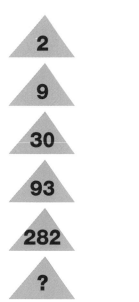

PUZZLE 12

Which number replaces the question mark and completes the puzzle?

2	1	9	7
2	7	4	4
3	3	7	5
4	0	9	?

102

What is missing from the last octagon?

Which letter completes the puzzle?

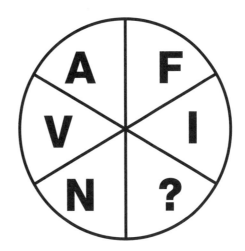

Which number replaces the question mark and completes the puzzle?

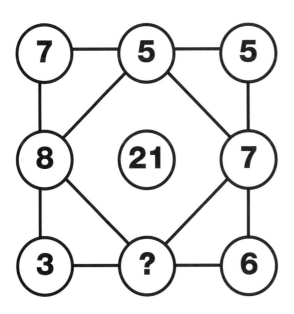

Where should the hour hand point to on the bottom clock?

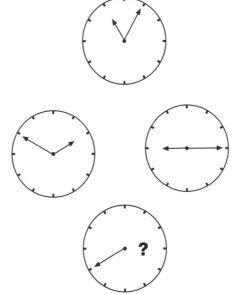

PUZZLE 17

What is missing from the last hexagon?

E   J   O   T   ?

PUZZLE 18

Which letter completes the puzzle?

B

C

E

H

?

PUZZLE 19

Which number replaces the question mark and completes the puzzle?

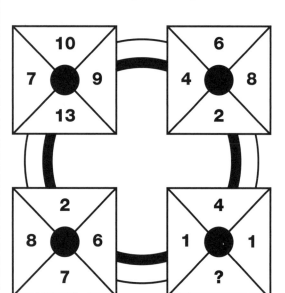

PUZZLE 20

Which number replaces the question mark and completes the chain?

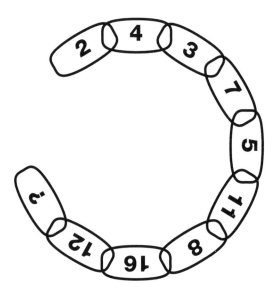

PUZZLE 21

What is missing from the last circle?

 E   **K**   **R**

 Z

 I   **S**   **?**

PUZZLE 22

Which number completes the puzzle?

 **1** **2**

 **2** **5** **?**

 **2** **1**

PUZZLE 23

Which number replaces the question mark and completes the puzzle?

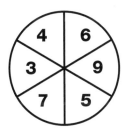
4	6
3	9
7	5

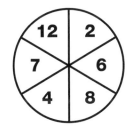
12	2
7	6
4	8

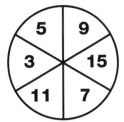
5	9
3	15
11	7

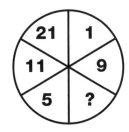
21	1
11	9
5	?

PUZZLE 24

Which number replaces the question mark and completes the puzzle?

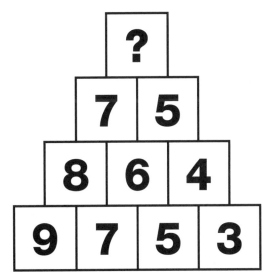

T
E
S
T

11

105

11

25 PUZZLE

What is missing from the last circle?

26 PUZZLE

Which letter replaces the question mark and completes the puzzle?

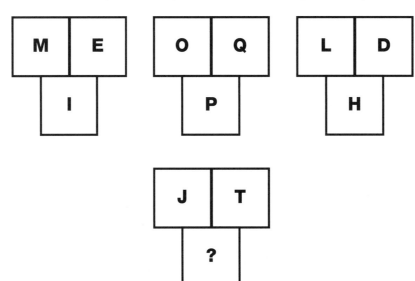

PUZZLE 27

What is missing from the last square?

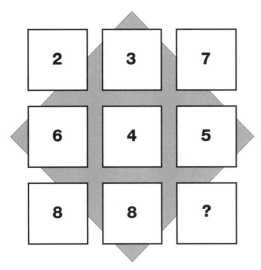

2	3	7
6	4	5
8	8	?

PUZZLE 28

Which letter completes the puzzle?

A	C	F	E	G	J
J	S	J	N	W	N
B	U	O	F	Y	S
D	F	I	K	M	P
M	V	M	T	C	T
E	X	R	L	E	?

PUZZLE 29

Which letter is the odd one out in each oval?

1
L
B P Q
T V

2
C
M S G
W D

PUZZLE 30

Which number replaces the question mark and completes the puzzle?

7	8	3
3	3	2
6	5	?

11

1 PUZZLE

Which letter replaces the question mark and completes the puzzle?

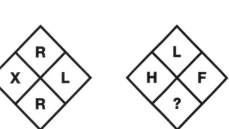

2 PUZZLE

Which number completes this puzzle?

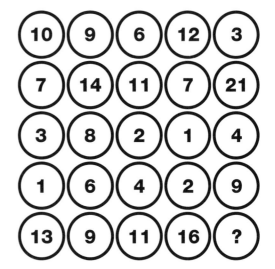

3 PUZZLE

Which letter will make this puzzle correct?

4 PUZZLE

Which letter replaces the question mark and completes the puzzle?

N	252	R
T	500	Y
Y	400	P
K	132	L
G	182	?

5 PUZZLE

Which letter replaces the question mark and completes the sequence?

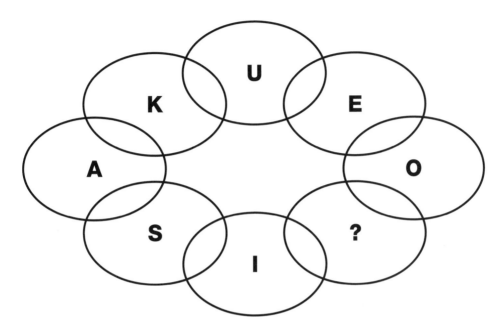

6 PUZZLE

Which number needs to be added to the final grid?

4	1	6	2
16	10	20	6
3	9	11	4

3	8	1	7
13	14	6	13
6	6	3	1

12	8	3	0
7	10	17	6
4	2	17	6

9	11	2	5
9	14	4	8
4	3	4	?

PUZZLE 7

Which number fills the centre of the last star to complete the puzzle?

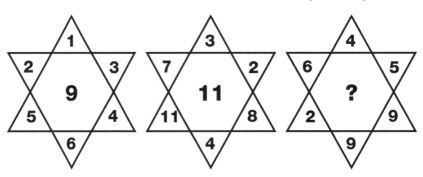

PUZZLE 8

Which letter replaces the question mark and completes the puzzle?

E		B
9	3	6
A		H

D		A
9	4	3
B		C

B		E
9	7	5
C		I

A		G
6	1	2
C		?

PUZZLE 9

Which number needs to be added to complete the puzzle?

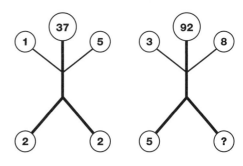

PUZZLE 10

Which letter replaces the question mark and completes the sequence?

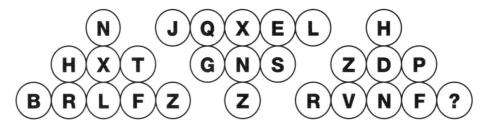

11 PUZZLE

Which number replaces the question mark and completes the puzzle?

7	12	8
1	4	6
3	11	11
9	11	5
12	13	?

12 PUZZLE

Which letter is missing from the bottom of the grid?

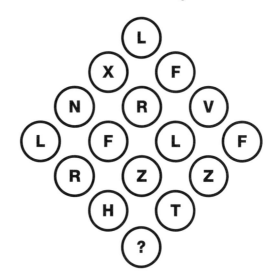

L

X   F

N   R   V

L   F   L   F

R   Z   Z

H   T

?

13 PUZZLE

Which number is missing from the bottom shape?

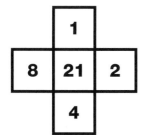

```
      2
   5 15 7
      5
```

```
      6
   4 19 11
      2
```

```
      1
   8 21 2
      4
```

```
      3
   8 23 6
      ?
```

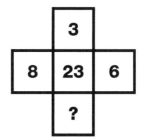

12

14 PUZZLE

Which number replaces the question mark and completes the sequence?

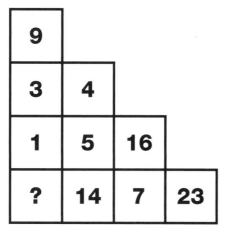

9			
3	4		
1	5	16	
?	14	7	23

15 PUZZLE

Which number replaces the question mark and completes the sequence?

9	3
13	7

21	6
8	9

31	33
31	53

16	13
9	10

7	9
3	?

16 PUZZLE

Which playing card replaces the question mark and completes the puzzle?

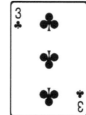

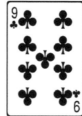

PUZZLE 17

Which letter replaces the question mark and completes the sequence?

B	G
K	F

L	Q
A	V

P	U
?	T

Z	E
O	J

PUZZLE 18

Which number replaces the question mark and completes the sequence?

0	6	4	1	2	1
1	2	5	1	4	4
2	1	6	1	6	9
3	4	3	1	9	6
5	1	2	2	2	5
7	2	9	2	5	?

PUZZLE 19

Where should the missing hour hand point to?

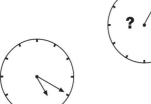

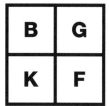

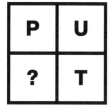

PUZZLE 20

Which letter replaces the question mark and completes the puzzle?

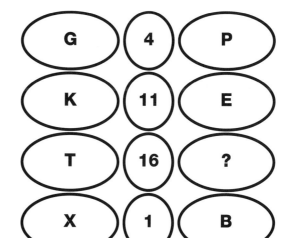

G | 4 | P

K | 11 | E

T | 16 | ?

X | 1 | B

TEST

12

PUZZLE 21

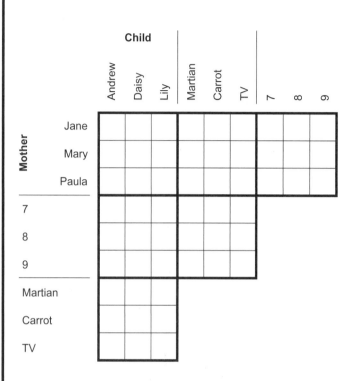

Andrew, Daisy and Lily were all excited about their school's fancy dress competition, and their mothers had spent a good deal of time getting their costumes ready. Jane's child (the youngest of the group) went dressed up as a TV set. Mary was so proud of her child, who is 9 years old. Andrew, whose mum is Paula, did not go as a Martian. Daisy loved Andrew's costume but, being younger than him, thought she looked sweeter in hers.

From all this information, can you tell the name of each child's mother, which costume each wore to the fancy dress competition, and the age of each child?

Child	Mother	Costume	Age

PUZZLE 22

Which letter replaces the question mark and completes the puzzle?

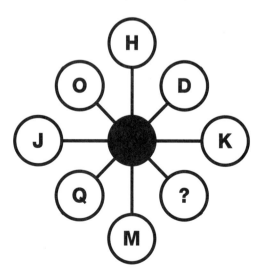

PUZZLE 23

Which letter replaces the question mark and completes the sequence?

A	EJP	W
Y U K		E N X
B	?MG	B

24 PUZZLE

Which picture cube does this shape make?

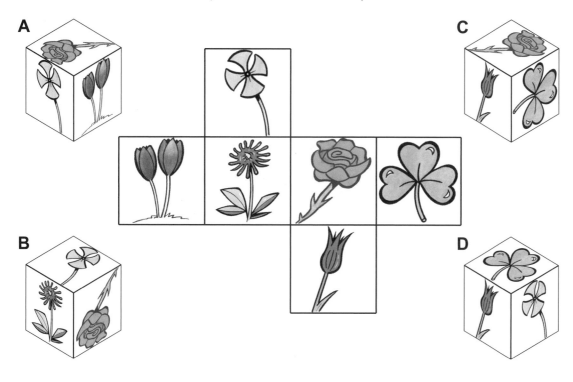

A

C

B

D

25 PUZZLE

Which letter replaces the question mark and completes the puzzle?

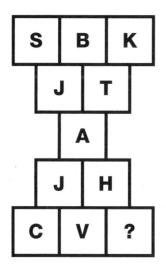

S	B	K
	J	T
	A	
J	H	
C	V	?

26 PUZZLE

If five men can dig 100 holes over four days, how many men would be needed to dig 150 holes in one day?

27 PUZZLE

Which number replaces the question mark and completes the puzzle?

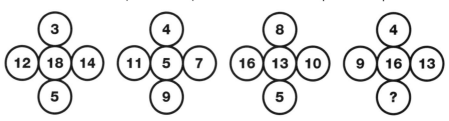

3
12 18 14
5

4
11 5 7
9

8
16 13 10
5

4
9 16 13
?

28 PUZZLE

Which letter replaces the question mark and completes the puzzle?

E Z
H W
L Q

D I
R O

V S
A N
G ?

29 PUZZLE

Which number replaces the question mark and completes the puzzle?

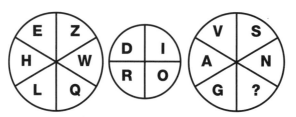

5	6	1
	5	
	4	

8	11	3
	24	
	5	

2	8	6
	12	
	4	

7	11	?
	28	
	3	

30 PUZZLE

What spot total should be shown where the question mark is?

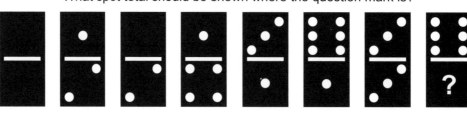

1 PUZZLE

What is missing from the last grid?

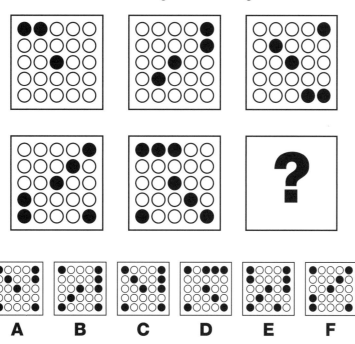

A   B   C   D   E   F

2 PUZZLE

Which watch completes the puzzle?

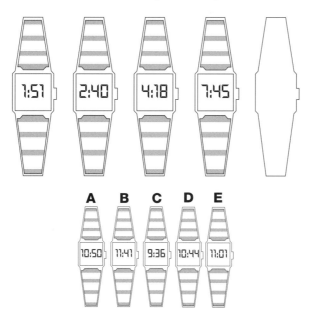

1:51   2:40   4:18   7:45

A   B   C   D   E
10:50   11:47   9:36   10:44   11:01

PUZZLE 3

Which of the lower circles is the missing one from the puzzle?

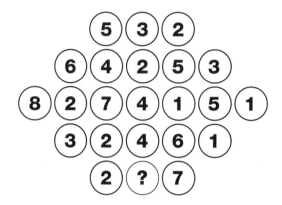

(5)(3)(2)
(6)(4)(2)(5)(3)
(8)(2)(7)(4)(1)(5)(1)
(3)(2)(4)(6)(1)
(2)(?)(7)

(1)(2)(3)(4)(5)(6)(7)(8)

PUZZLE 4

Which letter replaces the question mark and completes the puzzle?

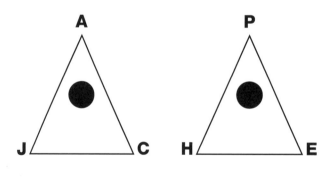

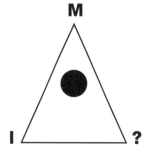

PUZZLE 5

What is missing from the last segment?

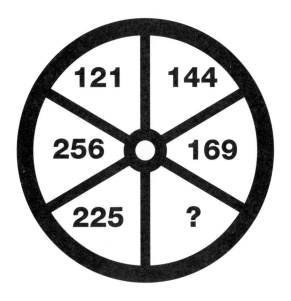

PUZZLE 6

Which letter completes the puzzle?

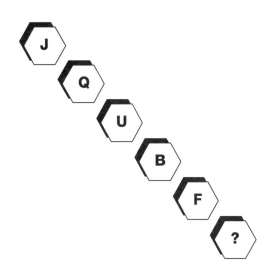

PUZZLE 7

Which number replaces the question mark and completes the puzzle?

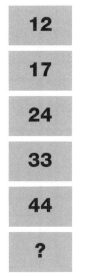

12
17
24
33
44
?

PUZZLE 8

Which number replaces the question mark and completes the puzzle?

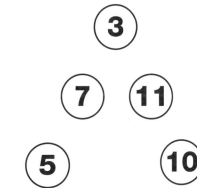

13

TEST

PUZZLE 9

What is missing from the last hexagon?

 B ?

PUZZLE 10

Which letter completes the puzzle?

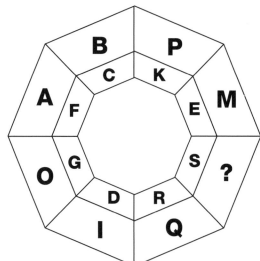

PUZZLE 11

Which number replaces the question mark and completes the puzzle?

7
9
13
21
37
?

PUZZLE 12

Which number replaces the question mark and completes the puzzle?

7	4	3	1
2	2	3	7
6	5	8	5
3	7	4	?

PUZZLE 13

What is missing from the last circle?

PUZZLE 14

Which letter completes the puzzle?

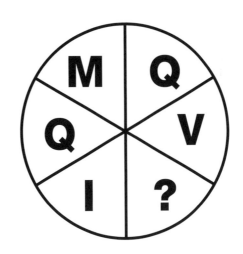

PUZZLE 15

Which number replaces the question
mark and completes the puzzle?

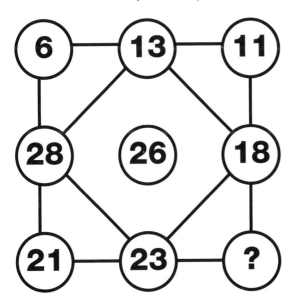

PUZZLE 16

Where should the minute hand
point to on the bottom clock?

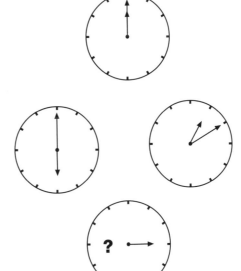

TEST

13

121

17 PUZZLE

What is missing from the last hexagon?

1 2 4 6 ?

18 PUZZLE

Which letter completes the puzzle?

B

C

D

G

?

19 PUZZLE

Which letter replaces the question mark and completes the puzzle?

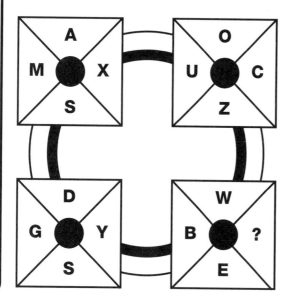

20 PUZZLE

Which number replaces the question mark and completes the chain?

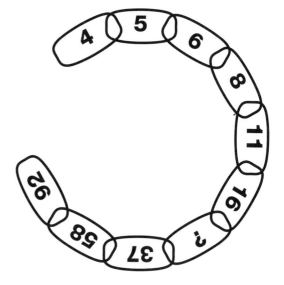

13

PUZZLE 21

What is missing from the last circle?

 N   S   T

 G

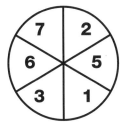 M   L   ?

PUZZLE 22

Which letter completes the puzzle?

 L   R

 G   P   ?

 C   G

PUZZLE 23

Which number replaces the question mark and completes the puzzle?

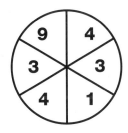

PUZZLE 24

Which letter replaces the question mark and completes the puzzle?

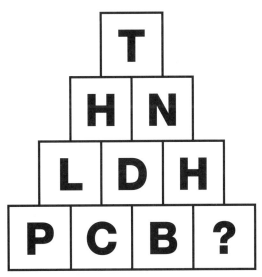

TEST

13

123

25 PUZZLE

Which letter replaces the question mark?

E J O T

Z S ? Y

U N I D

P K F A

26 PUZZLE

Which number replaces the question mark and completes the puzzle?

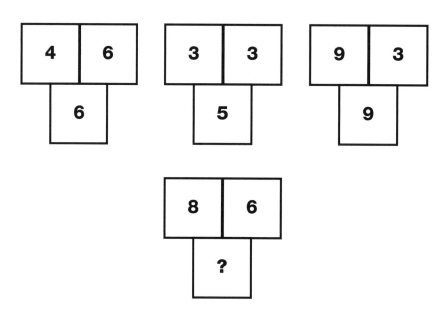

4	6
	6

3	3
	5

9	3
	9

8	6
	?

PUZZLE 27

What is missing from the last square?

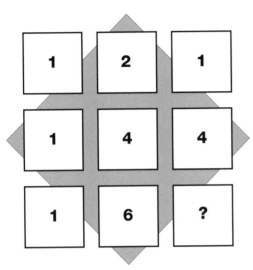

PUZZLE 28

Which letter completes the puzzle?

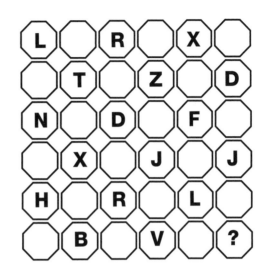

PUZZLE 29

Which number is the odd one out in each oval?

PUZZLE 30

Which number replaces the question mark and completes the puzzle?

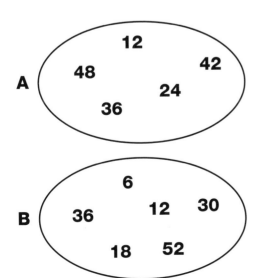

125

PUZZLE 1

Which number completes this wheel?

PUZZLE 2

Which number completes the puzzle?

PUZZLE 3

Where should the missing hour hand point to on the bottom clock face?

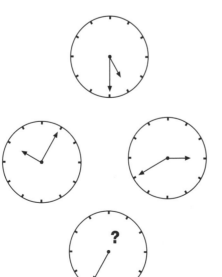

PUZZLE 4

Which letter replaces the question mark and completes the puzzle?

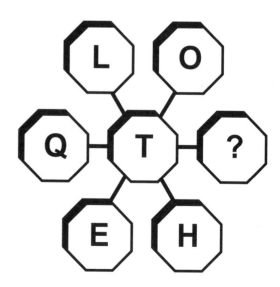

5 PUZZLE

What is missing from the lower middle circle?

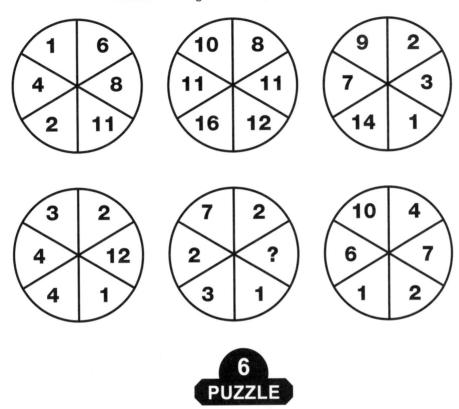

6 PUZZLE

Which letter replaces the question mark and completes the puzzle?

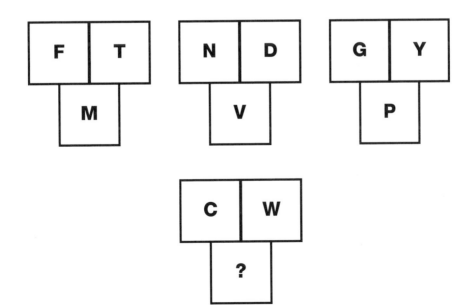

14

7 PUZZLE

What is missing from the last hexagon?

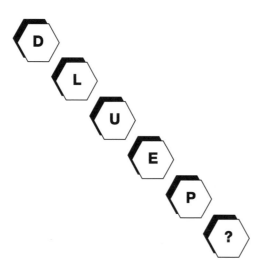

8 PUZZLE

Which number completes the puzzle?

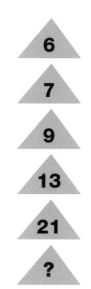

9 PUZZLE

Which letter replaces the question mark and completes the puzzle?

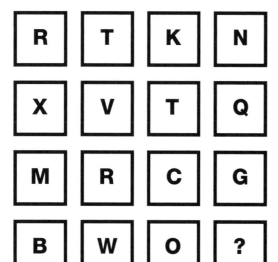

10 PUZZLE

Which letter replaces the question mark and completes the puzzle?

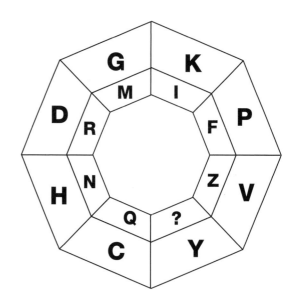

PUZZLE 11

What is missing from the last circle?

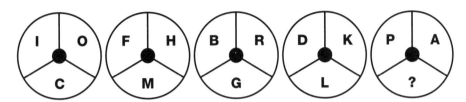

PUZZLE 12

Which letter replaces the question mark and completes the puzzle?

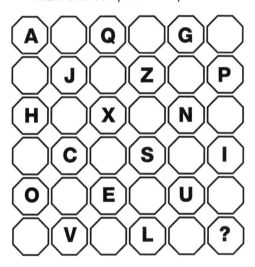

PUZZLE 13

Which number completes the puzzle?

PUZZLE 14

Which number replaces the question mark and completes the puzzle?

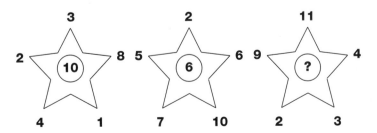

15 PUZZLE

Which letter replaces the question mark to complete the puzzle?

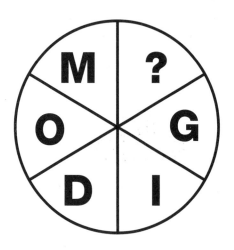

16 PUZZLE

Which number completes the puzzle?

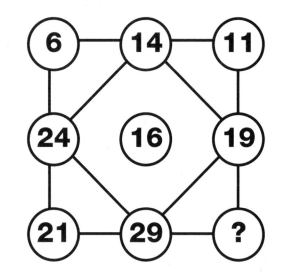

17 PUZZLE

Which of the lower patterns completes the puzzle?

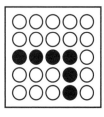
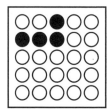
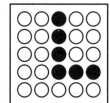

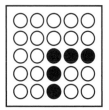
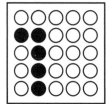

A   **B**   **C**   **D**   **E**   **F**

18 PUZZLE

What is missing from the last oval?

BGK

OFA

HIG

OCH

FQE

MI?

19 PUZZLE

Which number completes the puzzle?

20 PUZZLE

Which letter replaces the question mark and completes the puzzle?

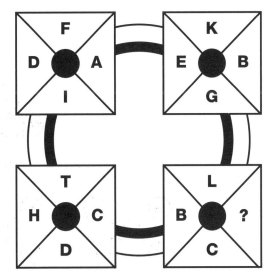

T
E
S
T

14

131

21 PUZZLE

Which letter is missing from the puzzle?

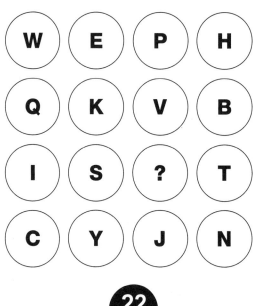

22 PUZZLE

Which number replaces the question mark and completes the puzzle?

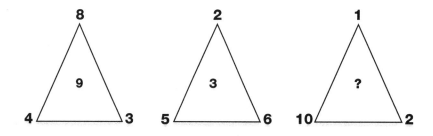

23 PUZZLE

Which letter completes the puzzle?

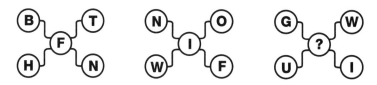

PUZZLE 24

What is missing from the last star?

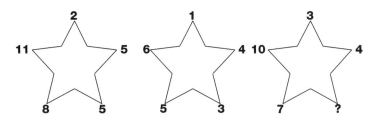

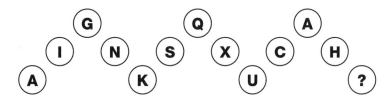

PUZZLE 25

Which letter completes the puzzle?

PUZZLE 26

Which number replaces the question mark and completes the puzzle?

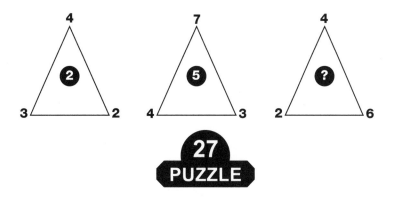

PUZZLE 27

Which number replaces the question mark and completes the puzzle?

28 PUZZLE

What time would the blank watch show?

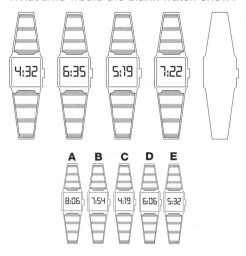

29 PUZZLE

Which letter replaces the question mark and completes the puzzle?

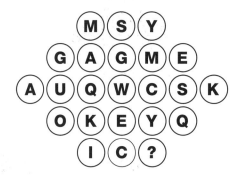

30 PUZZLE

Which letter replaces the question mark and completes the puzzle?

Which number replaces the question mark and completes the puzzle?

Which letter replaces the question mark and completes the grid?

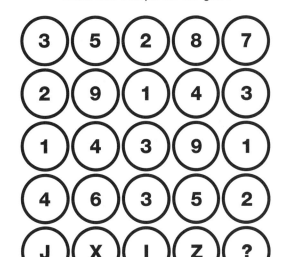

Which letter replaces the question mark and completes the wheel?

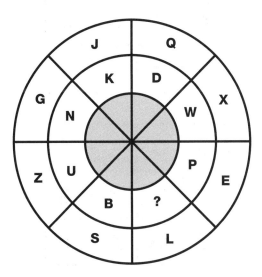

Which number replaces the question mark and completes the sequence?

6	FKM	24
12	LUC	24
20	IRB	9
4	DGQ	24
34	PJH	?

TEST

15

135

5 PUZZLE

What is missing from this puzzle?

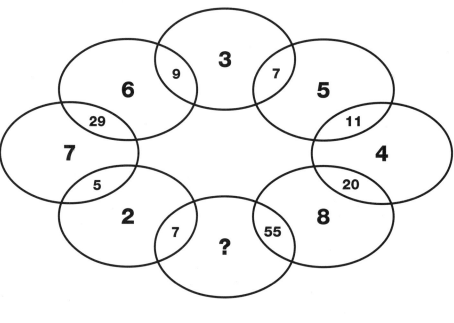

6 PUZZLE

Which letter replaces the question mark and completes the final grid?

D	C	H	G
I	X	M	B
N	S	R	W

R	V	B	F
X	P	H	Z
D	J	N	T

J	S	Z	I
Q	L	G	B
X	E	N	U

O	C	K	Y
W	U	?	Q
E	M	A	I

7 PUZZLE

Which number replaces the question mark in the third star?

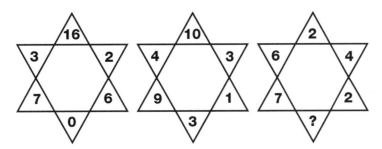

8 PUZZLE

Which letter replaces the question mark and completes the sequence?

J		N
E	P	E
A		W

B		F
W	H	W
S		O

Z		D
U	F	U
Q		M

S		W
N	Y	N
J		?

9 PUZZLE

Which number replaces the question mark on the head of the second figure?

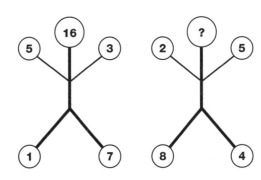

10 PUZZLE

Which number goes on top of the third triangle?

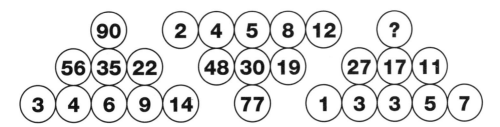

11 PUZZLE

Which number replaces the question mark and completes the puzzle?

1	2	1
4	4	1
9	6	1
6	9	1
5	2	?

12 PUZZLE

Which number completes this puzzle?

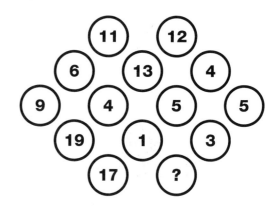

11 12
6 13 4
9 4 5 5
19 1 3
17 ?

13 PUZZLE

Which number replaces the question mark and completes the puzzle?

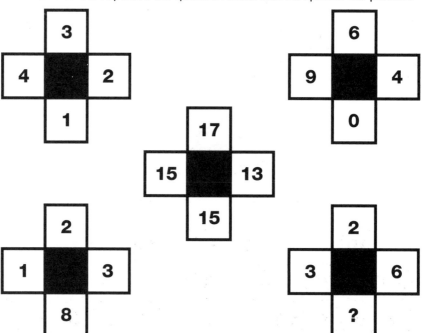

```
    3
  4   2
    1
```

```
    6
  9   4
    0
```

```
    17
 15    13
    15
```

```
    2
  1   3
    8
```

```
    2
  3   6
    ?
```

PUZZLE 14

Which letter replaces the question mark and completes the grid?

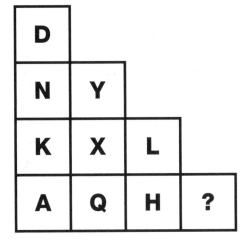

D			
N	Y		
K	X	L	
A	Q	H	?

PUZZLE 15

Which number replaces the question mark in the middle box?

3	1
2	7

0	1
6	6

4	12
12	?

9	5
6	1

5	2
0	3

PUZZLE 16

Which playing card replaces the question mark and completes the puzzle?

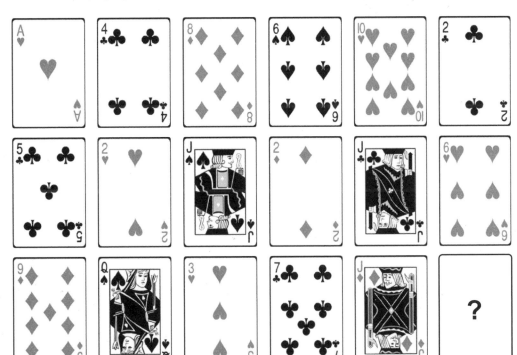

PUZZLE 17

Which letter replaces the question mark and completes the sequence?

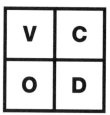

V	C
O	D

J	Q
F	X

H	H
A	Z

?	E
S	L

PUZZLE 18

Which letter replaces the question mark in this grid?

N		T		J	
	S		Y		O
R		X		D	
	W		C		I
L		B		H	
	Q		G		?

PUZZLE 19

What should the missing hand point to on the bottom clock?

PUZZLE 20

Which letter replaces the question mark and completes the grid?

53	J	49
82	X	37
36	L	15
14	?	98

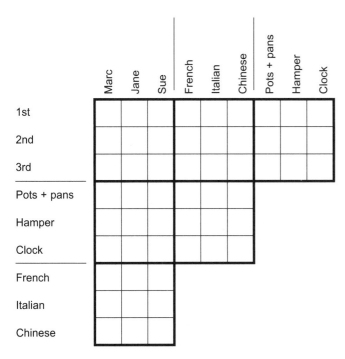

Marc, Jane and Sue were the three finalists in this year's Mastercook competition. The 2nd prize was awarded to the woman who prepared the Italian dish. The 3rd prize was the kitchen clock, but this didn't go to the person who prepared a grand Chinese meal. Sue won the hamper for her lovely meal, not the Italian dish.

From this information, can you work out each contestant's finishing position, the style of cooking he or she chose, and the prize he or she won?

Contestant	Position	Style	Prize

Which letter replaces the question mark at the bottom of the grid?

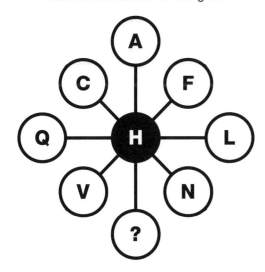

Which letter replaces the question mark and completes the grid?

B		C		E
?				G
Q		M		K

15

PUZZLE 24

Which picture cube does this shape make?

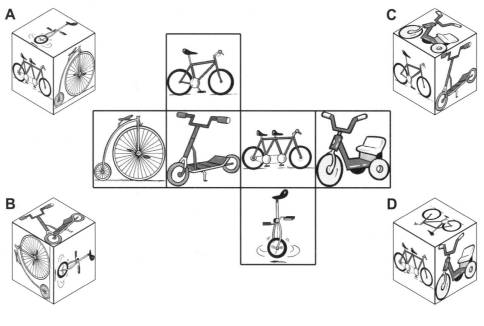

A

B

C

D

PUZZLE 25

Which letter replaces the question mark and completes the sequence?

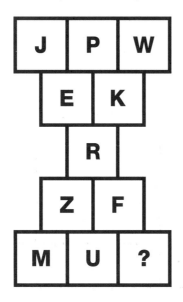

| J | P | W |
| E | K |
| R |
| Z | F |
| M | U | ? |

PUZZLE 26

Maria has a large climbing vine outside her house, which doubles in height every year. Since planting the vine six years ago, it has grown to 26 feet. How many years did it take to grow to half this height?

27 PUZZLE

Which letter replaces the question mark and completes the sequence?

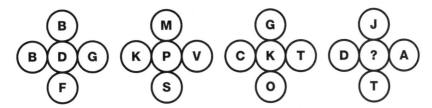

28 PUZZLE

Which number replaces the question mark in the last circle?

29 PUZZLE

Which letter replaces the question mark and completes the pattern?

J	Q	O		V	T	A		Y	F	D		K	I	P
	N				U				S				Z	
	X				E				C				?	

30 PUZZLE

What number should the last domino show on the bottom to complete this puzzle?

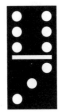

PUZZLE 1

What is missing from this wheel?

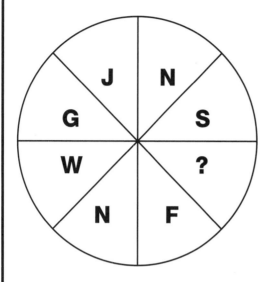

PUZZLE 2

Which letter completes the puzzle?

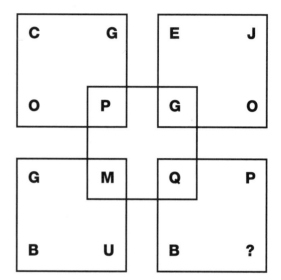

PUZZLE 3

Which symbol is needed to make the scales balance?

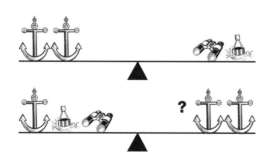

PUZZLE 4

Which number replaces the question mark and completes the puzzle?

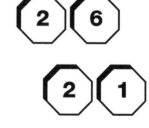

What is missing from the last circle?

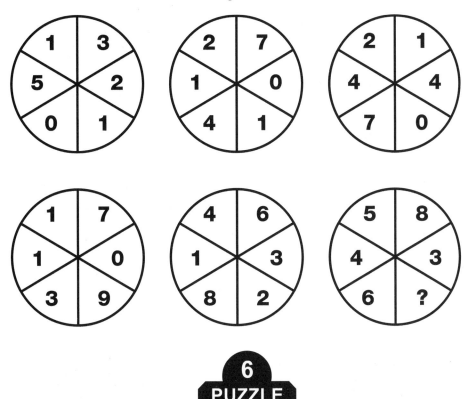

Which letter replaces the question mark and completes the puzzle?

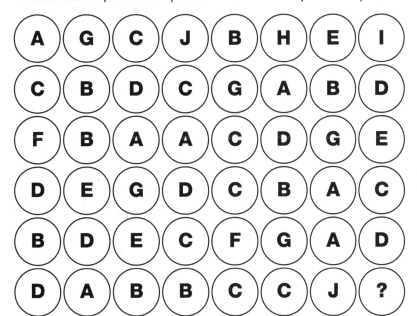

TEST

PUZZLE 7

What is missing from the middle circle?

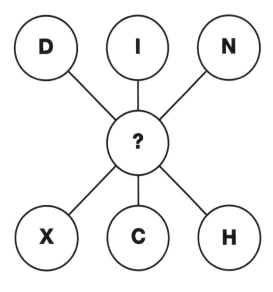

PUZZLE 8

Which number completes the puzzle?

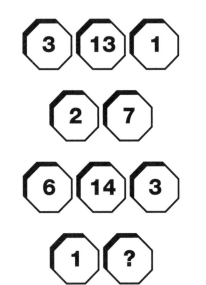

PUZZLE 9

Which number replaces the question mark and completes the puzzle?

5   12   26   54   ?

PUZZLE 10

Which number replaces the question mark and completes the puzzle?

156	
2	6
3	1
4	5
5	?

16

11 PUZZLE

What is missing from the last circle?

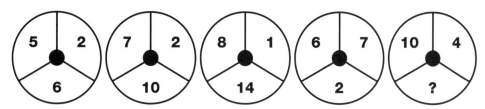

12 PUZZLE

Which number replaces the question mark and completes the puzzle?

6	1	5
3	9	10
4	3	?

13 PUZZLE

Which number completes the puzzle?

2 3 9

9 7

1 4 ?

14 PUZZLE

Which letter replaces the question mark and completes the puzzle?

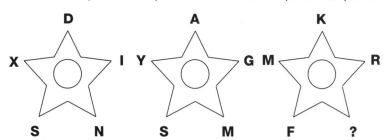

D
X   I Y   G
   S   N

A
      G M   R
   S   M

K
      R
   F   ?

15 PUZZLE

What is missing from the last circle?

C D K

G I F

J M ?

16 PUZZLE

Which number completes the puzzle?

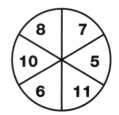

8 7
10 5
6 11

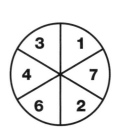

3 1
4 7
6 2

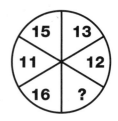

15 13
11 12
16 ?

17 PUZZLE

Which number replaces the question mark and completes the puzzle?

48	30	20
24	15	10
72	45	?

| 25 | 28 | 30 | 35 | 39 |

What is missing from the last oval?

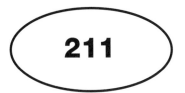

211

621

041

451

861

?

Which letter completes the puzzle?

A	J
X	M

D	G
S	P

B	E
S	P

Y	J
V	?

Which number replaces the question mark and completes the puzzle?

3	8
11	5
16	6
22	10
32	12
44	?

T
E
S
T

16

PUZZLE 21

Which of the bottom row of numbers replaces the question mark?

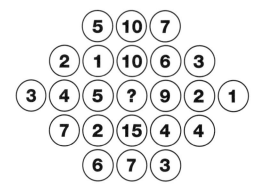

PUZZLE 22

Which letter replaces the question mark and completes the puzzle?

PUZZLE 23

Which number completes the puzzle?

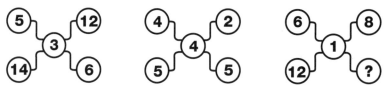

PUZZLE 24

What is missing from the last star?

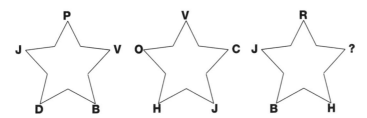

PUZZLE 25

Which letter completes the puzzle?

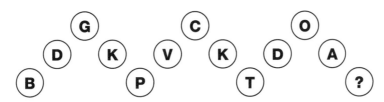

PUZZLE 26

Which letter replaces the question mark and completes the puzzle?

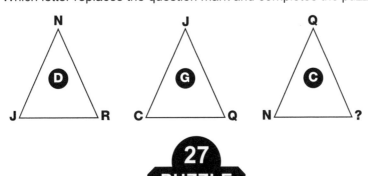

PUZZLE 27

Which number replaces the question mark and completes the puzzle?

PUZZLE 28

Which segment completes the puzzle?

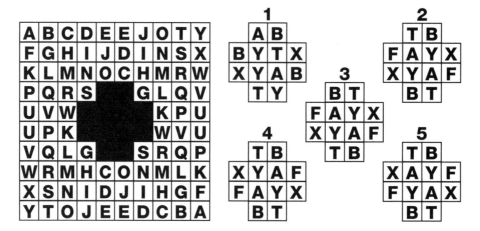

```
A B C D E E J O T Y
F G H I J D I N S X
K L M N O C H M R W
P Q R S ■ ■ G L Q V
U V W ■ ■ ■ K P U
U P K ■ ■ ■ W V U
V Q L G ■ ■ S R Q P
W R M H C O N M L K
X S N I D J I H G F
Y T O J E E D C B A
```

1
```
  A B
B Y T X
X Y A B
  T Y
```

2
```
  T B
F A Y X
X Y A F
  B T
```

3
```
  B T
F A Y X
X Y A F
  T B
```

4
```
  T B
X Y A F
F A Y X
  B T
```

5
```
  T B
X A Y F
F Y A X
  B T
```

PUZZLE 29

Which number replaces the question mark and completes the puzzle?

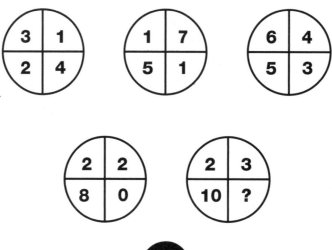

PUZZLE 30

Which letter replaces the question mark and completes the puzzle?

A H F K K N P ?

1
PUZZLE

Which grid continues the sequence?

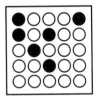

A   **B**   **C**   **D**   **E**   **F**

2
PUZZLE

Which of the bottom watches fills in the missing gap?

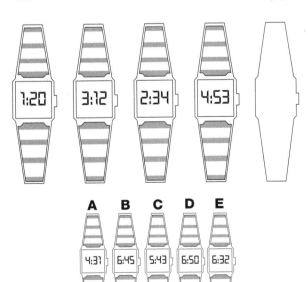

A   B   C   D   E

4:37   6:45   5:43   6:50   6:32

PUZZLE 3

Which of the lower letters replaces the question mark to complete the puzzle?

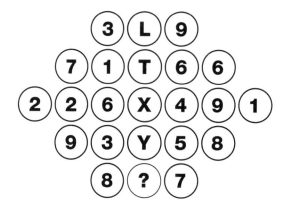

PUZZLE 4

Which number replaces the question mark and completes the puzzle?

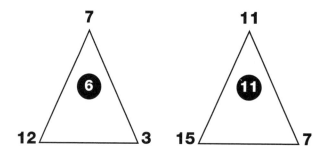

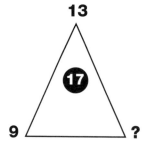

TEST

17

154

5 PUZZLE

What is missing from the last segment?

6 PUZZLE

Which number completes the puzzle?

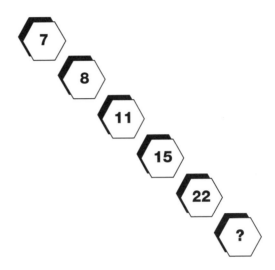

7 PUZZLE

Which letter replaces the question mark and completes the puzzle?

BG

CF

DE

ED

FC

G?

8 PUZZLE

Which letter replaces the question mark and completes the puzzle?

TEST

17

155

TEST

156

PUZZLE 9

What is missing from the last hexagon?

 6

 12

 15

 2

 4

 7

5

10

?

PUZZLE 10

Which letter completes the puzzle?

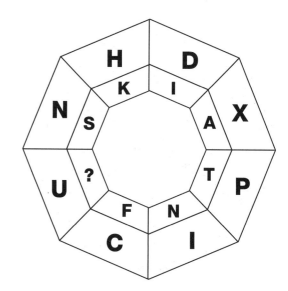

PUZZLE 11

Which letter replaces the question mark and completes the puzzle?

F
H
K
M
P
?

PUZZLE 12

Which number replaces the question mark and completes the puzzle?

1	3	4	1
2	0	4	8
2	7	5	5
3	4	6	?

PUZZLE 13

What is missing from the last octagon?

PUZZLE 14

Which letter completes the puzzle?

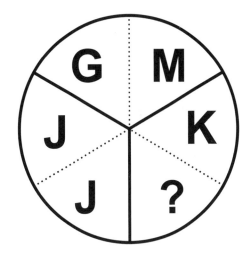

PUZZLE 15

Which number replaces the question mark and completes the puzzle?

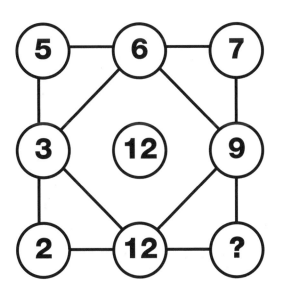

PUZZLE 16

Where should the minute hand point to on the bottom clock?

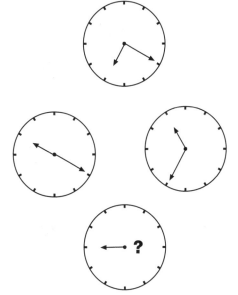

TEST

157

PUZZLE 17

What is missing from the last hexagon?

12 | 8 | 14 | 18 | ?

PUZZLE 18

Which number completes the puzzle?

26

22

18

12

?

PUZZLE 19

Which letter replaces the question mark and completes the puzzle?

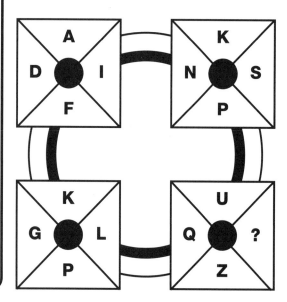

PUZZLE 20

Which number replaces the question mark and completes the chain?

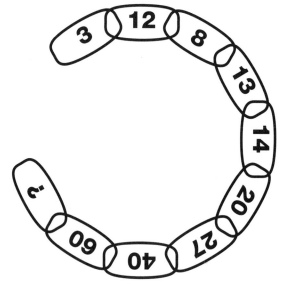

PUZZLE 21

What is missing from the last circle?

3   7   2

2

4   14   ?

PUZZLE 22

Which letter completes the puzzle?

I   O

M   F   ?

G   A

PUZZLE 23

Which number replaces the question mark and completes the puzzle?

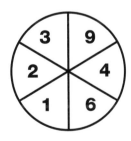 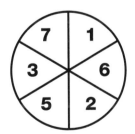

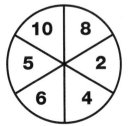 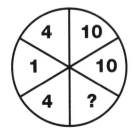

PUZZLE 24

Which number replaces the question mark and completes the puzzle?

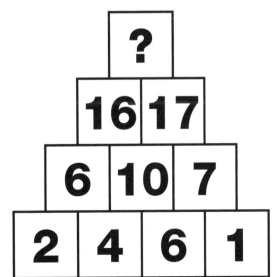

25 PUZZLE

What is missing from the last circle?

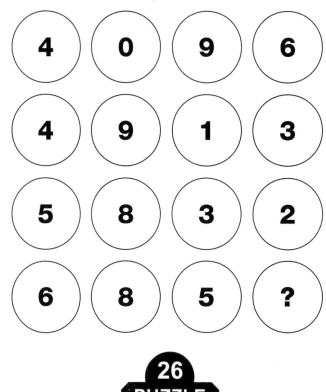

26 PUZZLE

Which letter replaces the question mark and completes the puzzle?

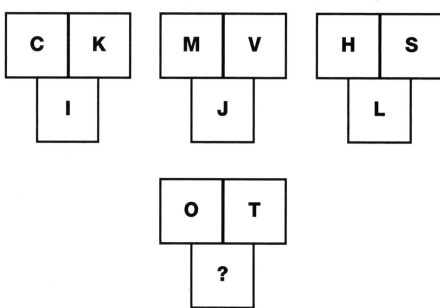

PUZZLE 27

What is missing from the last square?

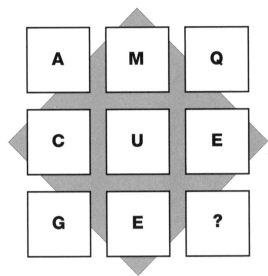

A	M	Q
C	U	E
G	E	?

PUZZLE 28

Which number completes the puzzle?

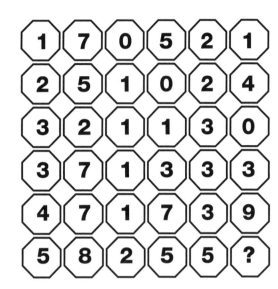

1	7	0	5	2	1
2	5	1	0	2	4
3	2	1	1	3	0
3	7	1	3	3	3
4	7	1	7	3	9
5	8	2	5	5	?

PUZZLE 29

Which two numbers are the odd ones out in these ovals?

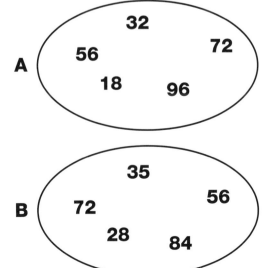

A: 32, 72, 56, 18, 96

B: 35, 56, 72, 28, 84

PUZZLE 30

Which number replaces the question mark and completes the puzzle?

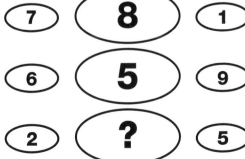

7	8	1
6	5	9
2	?	5

1 PUZZLE

Which number replaces the question mark and completes the puzzle?

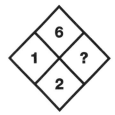
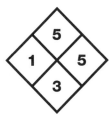
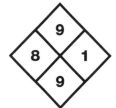

2 PUZZLE

Which number replaces the question mark and completes the grid?

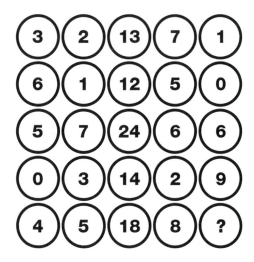

3 PUZZLE

Which number replaces the question mark and completes the wheel?

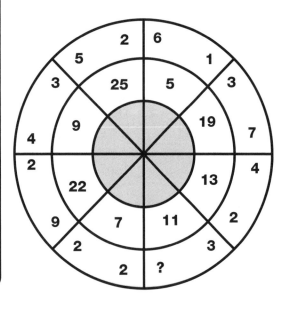

4 PUZZLE

Which number replaces the question mark and completes the puzzle?

3	GNQ	8
3	RBS	9
4	TUA	2
2	FPC	5
3	OLH	?

18

PUZZLE 5

Which letter replaces the question mark and completes the chain?

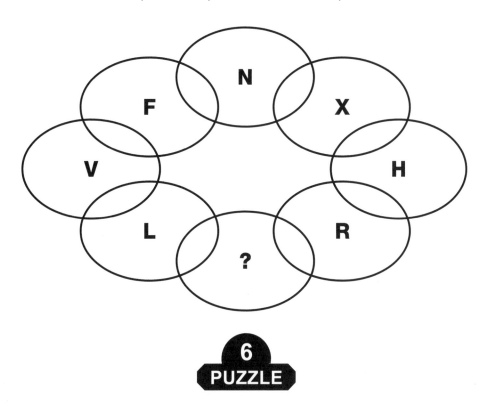

PUZZLE 6

Which number replaces the question mark in the bottom grid?

0	6	4	2
1	7	5	6
2	9	7	1

1	9	5	5
3	0	6	9
4	2	8	4

2	4	6	0
3	5	7	4
4	7	8	9

0	8	4	4
1	9	5	8
3	1	7	?

What is missing from the right hand star?

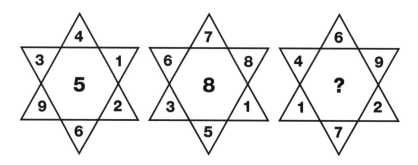

Which letter replaces the question mark and completes the puzzle?

Which number replaces the question mark in the second figure?

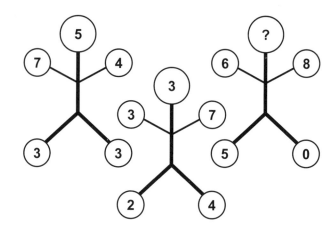

Which letter replaces the question mark in the third triangle?

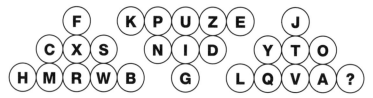

TEST

18

PUZZLE 11

Which letter replaces the question mark
and completes the sequence?

9	L	6
3	S	5
11	G	9
4	J	13
3	?	8

PUZZLE 12

Which letter replaces the question
mark in this formation?

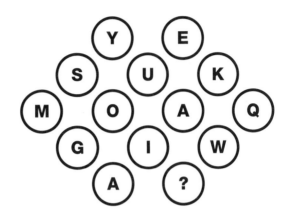

Y E
S U K
M O A Q
G I W
A ?

PUZZLE 13

Which number replaces the question mark and completes the puzzle?

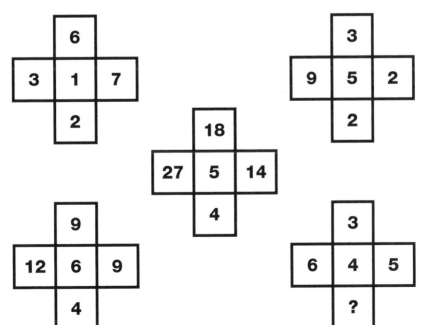

	6	
3	1	7
	2	

	3	
9	5	2
	2	

	18	
27	5	14
	4	

	9	
12	6	9
	4	

	3	
6	4	5
	?	

T E S T

18

14 PUZZLE

Which number replaces the question mark and completes the puzzle?

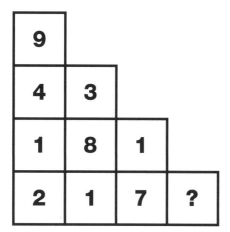

9			
4	3		
1	8	1	
2	1	7	?

15 PUZZLE

Which letter replaces the question mark and completes the last grid?

| A | J |
| L | R |

| Q | C |
| V | M |

| I | V |
| F | H |

| S | D |
| G | A |

| Z | V |
| ? | E |

16 PUZZLE

Which playing card replaces the question mark and completes the puzzle?

17 PUZZLE

Which number replaces the question mark and completes the puzzle?

4	2
6	11

7	8
2	3

10	9
7	13

4	7
5	?

18 PUZZLE

Which number replaces the question mark and completes the pattern?

3		23	6		7
	41			28	
7		8	2		13
4		19	14		3
	45			47	
17		5	11		?

19 PUZZLE

Where should the minute hand point to on the bottom clock?

20 PUZZLE

Which letter replaces the question mark and completes the puzzle?

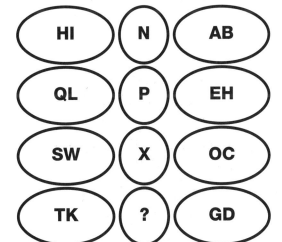

21 PUZZLE

	Anne	Beryl	Frank	Pete Shear	Max Morris	Lucy Carr	120 pages	250 pages	400 pages
Thriller									
Biography									
Romance									
120 pages									
250 pages									
400 pages									
Pete Shear									
Max Morris									
Lucy Carr									

Anne, Beryl and Frank are keen readers, and like nothing more than settling down with their favourite books. Beryl likes thrillers the best, but never reads anything which is longer than 300 pages. Anne's book, which is only 120 pages long, features Max Morris as its hero. Frank's book was a good read, but didn't feature Lucy Carr. The romantic novel did not feature Pete Shear. From this information, can you deduce which reader likes which kind of book, who was the central hero of the book they chose, and how many pages long the books were?

Reader	Book type	Hero	Book length

22 PUZZLE

Which letter replaces the question mark and completes the sequence?

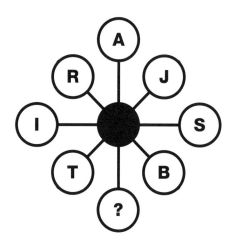

23 PUZZLE

Which number replaces the question mark and completes the grid?

4	8 3 2	8
5 7 4		2 3 3
5	6 1 4	?

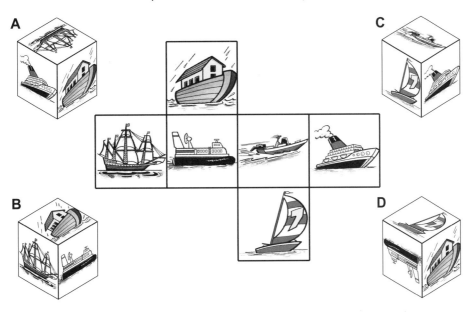

PUZZLE 24

Which picture cube does this shape make?

A

C

B

D

PUZZLE 25

Which letter replaces the blank and completes the sequence?

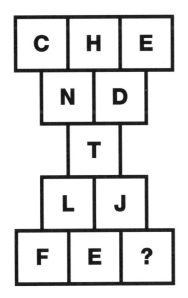

C H E
N D
T
L J
F E ?

PUZZLE 26

Patrick, Mark and Peter had spent the week decorating their elderly neighbour's house, for which they had earned £500 between them. When it came to dividing up the money, Patrick claimed he had worked three times harder than Mark, and Peter had worked twice as hard as Patrick. If the money was to be divided fairly, how much did each worker receive?

18

27 PUZZLE

Which number replaces the question mark and completes the puzzle?

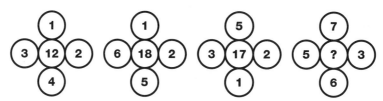

28 PUZZLE

Which number replaces the question mark and completes the puzzle?

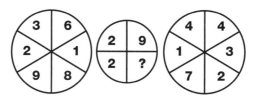

29 PUZZLE

Which number replaces the question mark and completes the puzzle?

3	6	2
	18	
	12	

4	5	1
	20	
	5	

6	4	5
	24	
	20	

3	7	8
	21	
	?	

30 PUZZLE

What should go on the top of the last domino?

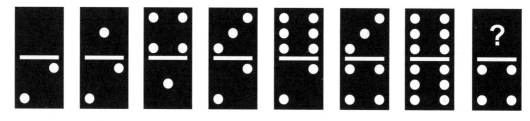

PUZZLE 1

What is missing in the last grid?

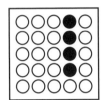
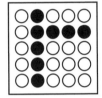

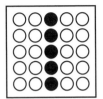
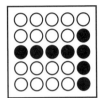

?

A **B** **C** **D** **E** **F**

PUZZLE 2

What time should the missing watch show?

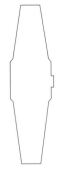

A **B** **C** **D** **E**

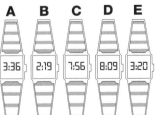

Which of the letters shown below replaces the question mark to complete the puzzle?

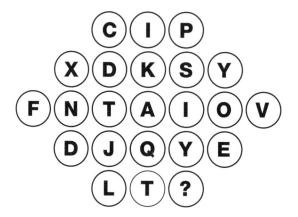

Which letter replaces the question mark and completes the puzzle?

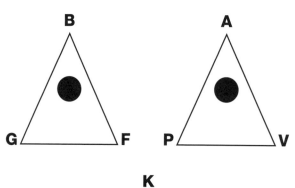

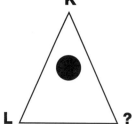

Sidebar:

T E S T

19

172

PUZZLE 5

What is missing from the last segment?

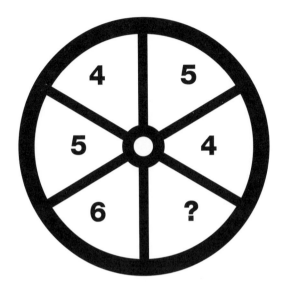

PUZZLE 6

Which number replaces the question mark and completes the puzzle?

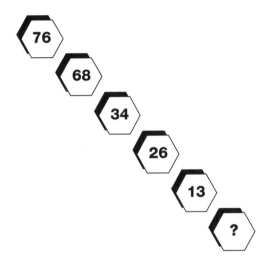

PUZZLE 7

Which number replaces the question mark and completes the puzzle?

44

69

96

25

56

?

PUZZLE 8

Which letter replaces the question mark and completes the puzzle?

G

J ?

N W

S Y F N

PUZZLE 9

What is missing from the last hexagon?

7 11 2

6 14 4

5 19 ?

PUZZLE 10

Which letter completes the puzzle?

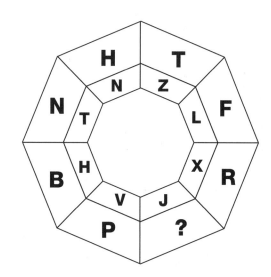

PUZZLE 11

Which number replaces the question mark and completes the puzzle?

8

12

17

23

30

?

PUZZLE 12

Which number replaces the question mark and completes the puzzle?

3	1	2	4
7	2	6	7
3	5	2	8
4	4	2	?

What is missing from the last octagon?

Which letter completes the puzzle?

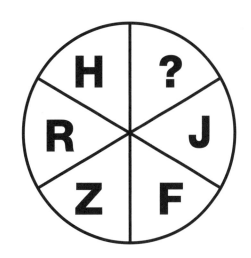

Which number replaces the question mark and completes the puzzle?

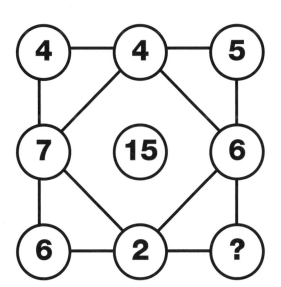

Where should the missing hand point to?

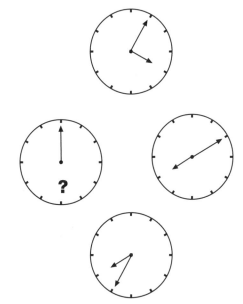

PUZZLE 17

What is missing from the last hexagon?

⬡ 8 ⬡ 16 ⬡ 11 ⬡ 22 ⬡ ?

PUZZLE 18

Which letter completes the puzzle?

A

D

E

I

?

PUZZLE 19

Which letter replaces the question mark and completes the puzzle?

F
A ● B
J

N
S ● P
Z

O
C ● J
U

M
C ● ?
A

PUZZLE 20

Which number replaces the question mark and completes the chain?

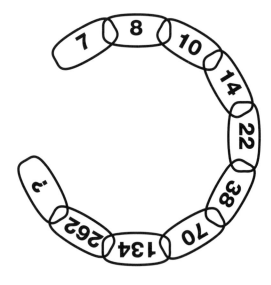

7 8 10 14 22 38 70 134 262 ?

21 PUZZLE

What is missing from the last circle?

D   J   M

S

V   B   ?

22 PUZZLE

Which letter completes the puzzle?

D   B

A   A   G

G   ?

23 PUZZLE

Which number replaces the question mark and completes the puzzle?

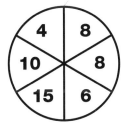 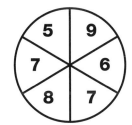

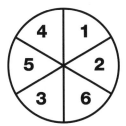 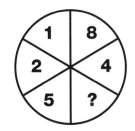

24 PUZZLE

Which number replaces the question mark and completes the puzzle?

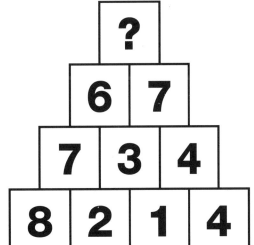

25 PUZZLE

What is missing from the last circle?

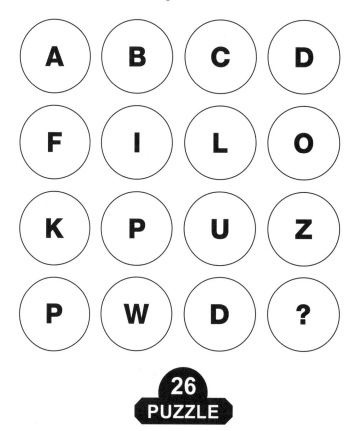

A	B	C	D
F	I	L	O
K	P	U	Z
P	W	D	?

26 PUZZLE

Which letter replaces the question mark and completes the puzzle?

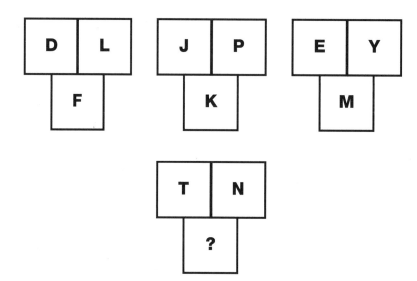

D	L
	F

J	P
	K

E	Y
	M

T	N
	?

PUZZLE 27

What is missing from the last square?

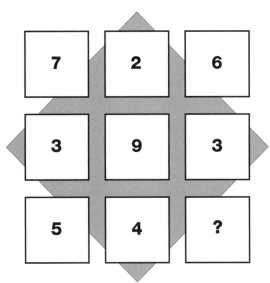

PUZZLE 28

Which letter completes the puzzle?

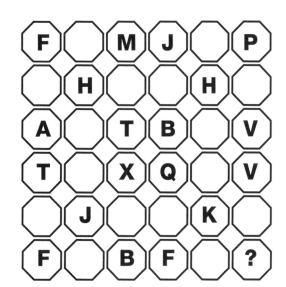

PUZZLE 29

Which numbers are the odd ones out in these two ovals?

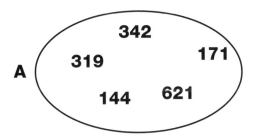

A

342
319   171
144   621

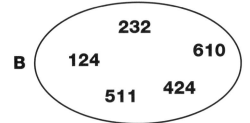

B

232
124   610
511   424

PUZZLE 30

Which letter replaces the question mark and completes the puzzle?

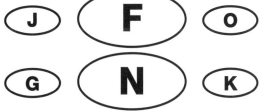

J   F   O

G   N   K

L   I   ?

PUZZLE 1

Which letter is missing from this puzzle?

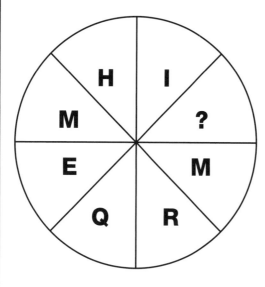

PUZZLE 2

Which letter completes the puzzle?

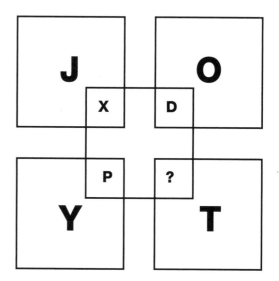

PUZZLE 3

Which number replaces the question mark and completes the puzzle?

71

79

67

80

68

?

PUZZLE 4

Which number replaces the question mark and completes the puzzle?

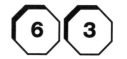

T E S T

20

180

5
PUZZLE

What is missing from the last circle?

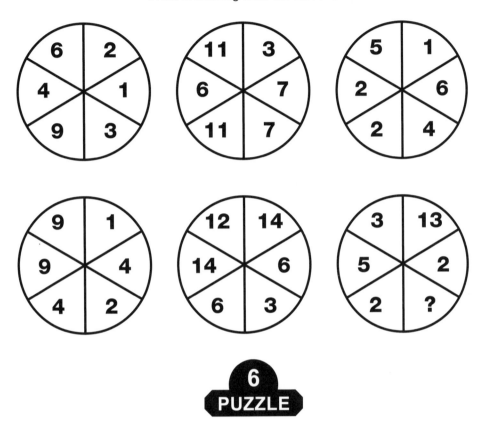

6
PUZZLE

Which letter replaces the question mark and completes the puzzle?

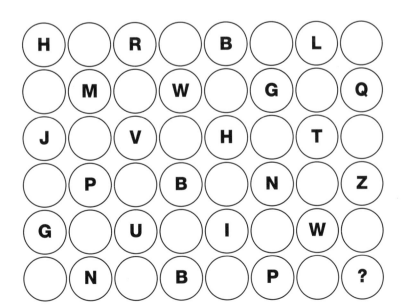

20

181

PUZZLE 7

What is missing from the middle circle?

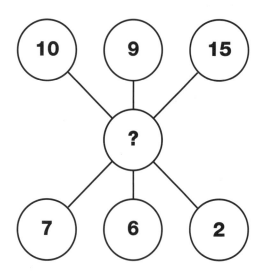

PUZZLE 8

Which letter completes the puzzle?

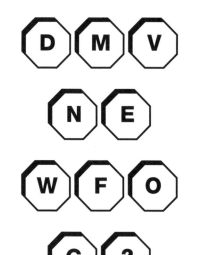

PUZZLE 9

Which number replaces the question mark and completes the puzzle?

| 5 | 6 | 9 | 16 | ? |

PUZZLE 10

Which number replaces the question mark and completes the puzzle?

PUZZLE 11

Which number is missing from the last circle?

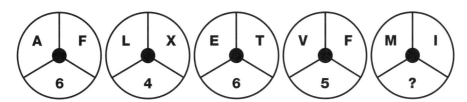

PUZZLE 12

Which number replaces the question mark and completes the puzzle?

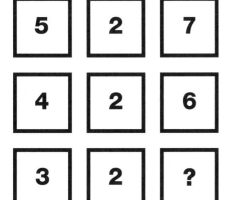

PUZZLE 13

Which letter completes the puzzle?

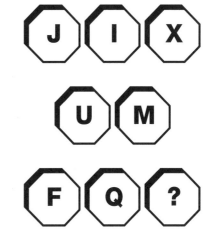

PUZZLE 14

Which number replaces the question mark and completes the puzzle?

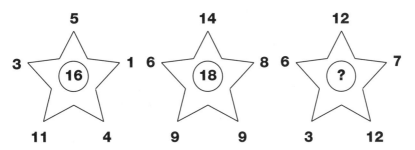

PUZZLE 15

What is missing from the last circle?

2	6	8
3	7	3
6	4	?

PUZZLE 16

Which letter completes the puzzle?

PUZZLE 17

Which number replaces the question mark and completes the puzzle?

6	2	17
1	4	11
3	7	?

| 9 | 11 | 13 | 17 | 21 |

18 PUZZLE

Which letters are missing from the last oval?

AJM

HOT

MVY

TAF

YHK

?

19 PUZZLE

Which letter completes the puzzle?

20 PUZZLE

Which numbers replace the question mark and complete the puzzle?

8	11
14	10
19	16
30	21
46	32
?	?

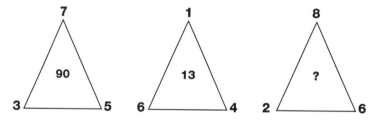

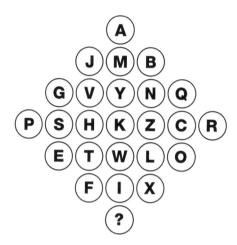
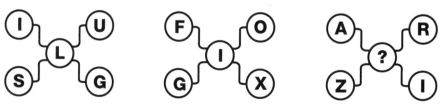

PUZZLE 21

Which of the lower letters replaces the question mark to complete this puzzle?

A
J M B
G V Y N Q
P S H K Z C R
E T W L O
F I X
?

A C G J N Q U X

PUZZLE 22

Which number replaces the question mark and completes the puzzle?

7
90
3   5

1
13
6   4

8
?
2   6

PUZZLE 23

Which letter completes the puzzle?

I   U
L
S   G

F   O
I
G   X

A   R
?
Z   I

PUZZLE 24

What is missing from the last star?

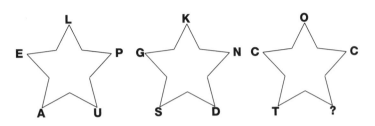

PUZZLE 25

Which letter completes the puzzle?

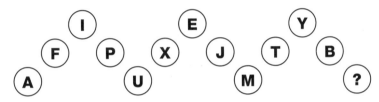

PUZZLE 26

Which number replaces the question mark and completes the puzzle?

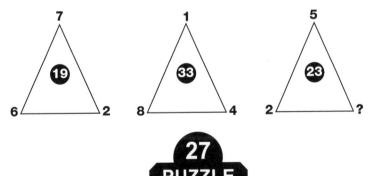

PUZZLE 27

Which letter replaces the question mark and completes the puzzle?

Which segment fills the missing gap to complete the puzzle?

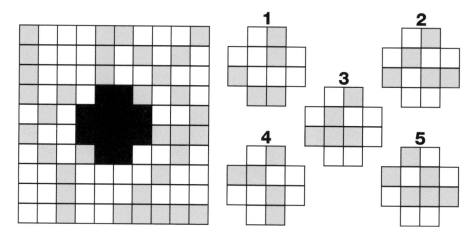

1

2

3

4

5

Which number replaces the question mark and completes the puzzle?

8	7
10	10

12	12
9	21

4	1
8	4

2	4
1	7

6	3
9	?

Which number replaces the question mark and completes the puzzle?

4   **7**   **15**   **31**   **35**   **19**   **11**   **?**

T E S T

20

SOLUTIONS

1 - D
The number of black dots in each grid increases by 1 each time, starting with the top left grid and working to the right, top row then bottom row.

2 - A
Starting with the watch on the left, add 42 minutes to the time shown to give the time on the next watch to the right.

3 - 6
Looking at the diagram in rows, the central circle equals half the sum of the numbers in the other circles to the left and right of the centre.

4 - 9
The number at the centre of each triangle equals the sum of the lower two numbers minus the top number.

5 - E
Starting with Y and moving clockwise, letters move backwards through the alphabet in steps of 2 letters, then 3 then 4 etc.

6 - 19
As you move diagonally down, numbers follow the sequence of Prime Numbers.

7 - V
As you move down the diagram, letters move through the alphabet in steps of 4.

8 - 16
Starting bottom left and moving clockwise around the triangle, numbers follow the sequence of Square Numbers.

9 - M
Working in rows, add together the numerical values of the left and right hand letters to give the numerical value of the central letter.

10 - O
In each segment of the diagram are a pair of letters, one of which is the same distance from the start of the alphabet as the other is from the end.

11 - 39
Working from top to bottom, double each number and subtract 1, then 2, then 3 etc.

12 - 4
Working in columns, the sum of the numbers in each column is always 14.

13 - V
Starting at the top left, and moving clockwise in a spiral towards the centre, letters move through the alphabet in steps of 5.

14 - K
The numerical values of the letters in opposite segments of the circle always add up to 17.

15 - 6
The numbers in each row and column add up to 15.

16 - Hand pointing to 5
Starting with the top clock and moving anti-clockwise around the others, the hour hand moves back 1 hour, then 2, then 3 etc, while the minute hand moves forward 10 minutes each time.

17 - 40
Moving from left to right, numbers increase by 2,3,4 and 5.

18 - K
As you move down, the numerical value of the letters follows the sequence of Prime Numbers.

19 - 9
In each square of the diagram, the sum of the numbers is always 22.

20 - 16
Moving clockwise, around alternate segments in the chain, one sequence decreases by 1, 2, 3 and 4 each time, while the other increases by 2, 3, 4 and 5.

21 - 7
Starting with the numbers in the top row, and following straight lines through the centre of the diagram, subtract the middle number from the top number to give the corresponding value on the bottom row.

22 - A
Writing each letter as its numerical value and working in rows, add the top 2-digit number to the bottom 2-digit number to give the 3-digit result in the centre.

23 - 13
In each circle, starting at the top left segment, numbers increase, as you move clockwise, by 2 for the upper left circle, 3 for the upper right, 4 for the lower right and 5 for the lower left.

24 - G
The numerical values of the letters in each row add up to 26 each time.

25 - W
Starting at the top left and moving down, then right one column and up etc in a snakes and ladders pattern, letters move through the alphabet 4 letters at a time.

26 - 3
In each group of 3 numbers, the lower number equals the average of the top two numbers.

27 - 1
Reading each row as a 3-digit number, the rows follow the sequence of square numbers, from 17 to 19.

28 - 8,1
Reading each row as 3 separate 2-digit numbers, the central number equals the average of the left and right hand numbers.

29 - A:58 B:86
In the first oval, all numbers are multiples of 8, and in the second, they are all multiples of 7.

30 - B
In each row, add the numerical value of the left and right hand letters together and write the letter with the reverse alphabetical value in the centre.

SOLUTIONS

1 - T
Starting at F and moving anti-clockwise, letters move through the alphabet in steps of 2, 3, 4, 5 etc.

2 - Q
Adding the three numbers in each outer square together gives the numerical value of the letter in the centre square.

3 - One hammer
The Hammer = 1, the File = 3 and the Axe = 5

4 - 1
Reading each pair of numbers as a 2-digit number, they follow the sequence of square numbers from 6 to 9.

5 - 7
Taking the top row of circles, numbers in the central circle equal the sum of the numbers in corresponding segments of the left and right hand circles. In the bottom row, numbers in the central circle equal the difference between numbers in corresponding segments of the left and right hand circles.

6 - P
Starting at the top left circle, and moving right, then down one row and moving left, in a snakes and ladders pattern, letters move through the alphabet in steps of 2, 3 and 4, repeating this pattern all the way down.

7 - 253
Starting at the top left, and moving through the diagram in a Z shape, double each number and add 3 to give the next number along. Alternatively, double the difference between each number, then add 4, 8, 16, 32, 64 and 128.

8 - U
Multiply the numerical values of the letters in each pair to give the 3-digit result in the spaces above.

9 - 51
Moving to the right, double each number and subtract 3 to give the next number along. Alternatively, double the difference between each number, then add 3, 6, 12, and 24.

10 - 2
Starting with the 10 at the top, one set of numbers increases by 3 each time, written in alternate boxes as you zigzag down the diagram, and the other set of numbers decreases by 2, written in the boxes remaining.

11 - I
Working from left to right, letters in corresponding segments of the circles move through the alphabet in steps of 2, 3 and 4, with their relative positions moving one place clockwise at each step.

12 - 6
On each row, add the values of the left hand and central boxes to give the value in the right hand box.

13 - V
Starting at the top left, and moving anti-clockwise around the figure, letters advance through the alphabet 5 letters at a time.

14 - 10
In each star diagram, the number in the centre equals the sum of the top three numbers, subtracting the sum of the bottom two numbers.

15 - 23
Starting top left, and moving down in columns from left to right, the numbers follow the sequence of Prime Numbers from 2 to 23.

16 - 10
Numbers in the segments of the left hand circle equal the difference between numbers in corresponding segments of the two right hand circles.

17 - E
Using the numerical value of each letter, in each column, the value of the central letter equals the sum of the values of the top and bottom letters.

18 - 1,143
Starting with the top 3-digit number, the first digit increases by 2 as you descend, from 1 to 11. The middle digit decreases by 1 each time, and the right hand digit alternates between 5 and 3.

19 - 6
Numbers in the lower left circle equal the sum of the numbers in corresponding segments of the top two circles, and numbers in the lower right circle equal the difference of the numbers in corresponding segments of the top two circles.

20 - N
The alphabetical value of the letters in the left hand column follows through the sequence of Prime Numbers, with the letters in the right hand column representing the corresponding reverse alphabetical values.

21 - I
Starting on the left, and moving downwards in columns from left to right, letters are written in alphabetical sequence, in steps of 4 letters at a time.

22 - 4
In each triangle, the central number equals the sum of the three outer numbers divided by two.

23 - B
In each diagram, letters are written in sequence, starting in the top left circle and moving clockwise around the other 3 outer circles, in steps given by the numerical value of the central letter each time.

24 - 5
In each star, the central number equals the difference between the sum of the even numbers and the sum of the odd numbers from the points of the star.

25 - U
Starting on the left, and moving along the line to the right, letters follow the alphabetic sequence, in steps of 2, 3, 4 and then 1, before repeating the sequence.

26 - 5
In each triangle, the number at the apex of the triangle equals the average of the two numbers at the bottom.

27 - 22
In each circle, the lower number equals the product of the top two numbers, subtracting 3 for the left hand circle, 4 for the middle, and 5 for the right hand circle.

28 - 2
Splitting the large square into quarters, each quarter features the same pattern of letters.

29 - Y
Starting in the top left circle, and following a W pattern through the others, letters in corresponding segments of the circles follow the alphabetical sequence in steps of 4 letters. Alternatively, the top two letters in each circle increase in value by 9, the bottom two by 7.

30 - W
Working from left to right, letters move forwards 7 places, then back 2. Repeat this sequence until the end.

SOLUTIONS

TEST 3

1 - 4
In each diamond, add the left and right hand numbers together, and subtract this sum from the top number to give the value at the bottom.

2 - 7
In each row of the diagram, the central value equals the sum of the differences between the left hand pair of numbers and the right hand pair of numbers.

3 - 7
The inner digit in each segment equals the sum of the two numbers in the outer part of the opposite segment.

4 - K
In each row, the product of the left and right hand numbers equals the sum of the numerical values of the three letters.

5 - H
Start at the top and move down, taking single letters or pairs of letters that appear on the same horizontal line. The sum of the numerical values of the letters in each line increases by 2 as you go down, from 18 to 26.

6 - 0
In each row of each grid, multiply the left and right hand numbers together to give a digit value, and write this value in the two centre boxes.

7 - F
In each star shape, the sum of the numerical values of the letters bounded by one triangle is equal to that of the other triangle.

8 - 5
In each H shape, the central number is equal to the difference between the sum of the 3 left hand numbers and the sum of the 3 right hand numbers.

9 - E
In each stick-man diagram, start on the left foot and move around the other limbs in a clockwise direction. The letters advance through the alphabet in steps given by the numerical value of the letter on the head of the diagram.

10 - B
Add together the numerical values of the letters in corresponding positions on the left and right hand triangles, and put the letter with this value in corresponding vertical mirror image positions of the centre triangle.

11 - 7
Reading each row of the diagram as a series of 3-digit numbers, the centre 3-digit number equals the sum of the top 2 numbers, and the sum of the lower 2 numbers.

12 - A
Start on the centre left of the diagram, and move in a clockwise spiral towards the centre. Letters advance through the alphabet in steps of 2, 3, 4, etc.

13 - 22
Add together values in corresponding positions of the top two crosses, and put the results in the lower left cross. Calculate the difference between values in corresponding positions of the top two crosses, and put the results in the lower right cross. Finally, add together the values in corresponding positions of the lower two crosses to give the values in the central cross.

14 - T
Working through the diagram in columns, left to right, The sum of the numerical values of the letters in each column follows the sequence 17, 18, 19 and 20.

15 - 2
Start with the top left hand box, and move around the others in a clockwise spiral towards the centre. Read each box as a pair of 2-digit numbers, one above the other. The sum of the 2-digit numbers in each box follows the sequence 55, 60, 65, 70 and 75.

16 - 9 of Clubs
Taking red cards as positive values and black cards as negative values, in each column of the diagram, the lower card value equals the sum of the two upper card values.

17 - Z
Read the diagram as a whole grid of 4x4 squares. Starting on the bottom left square, move clockwise around the outside of the whole square, with letters written in sequence, skipping 4 letters at a time. Repeat this instruction for the small inner square.

18 - X
Start at the top left and move in alternate boxes from left to right, then down one row and to the left, in a snakes and ladders pattern. Letters advance through the alphabet in steps of 2, 3, 4...8, before repeating this pattern.

19 - To the 4
Start with the top left clock-face, and move around the others in a clockwise direction. The value pointed to by the hour hand is four places anticlockwise of the minute hand, then five places anticlockwise of the minute hand, then six places, etc.

20 - H
In each row, the numerical value of the central letter equals the difference between the sum of the numerical values of the two left hand letters and the sum of the numerical values of the two right hand letters.

21 -

Owner	Property	Road	Value
Mavis	Flat	Shangri-La Way	£75,000
Harold	Bungalow	Meadow Rise	£100,000
Bette	Terrace	Honeysuckle Row	£40,000

22 - C
Start on the far left of the diagram and move around it in a clockwise direction. Letters advance through the alphabet in steps of 8 then 9, repeating this pattern all the way around.

23 - 12
The value at each corner of the diagram equals the difference between the sums of the numerical values of the letters in the boxes adjacent to the corner.

24 - C

25 - E
Working through the diagram in rows, from top to bottom, the sum of the numerical values of the letters in each row follows the sequence 15, 20, 25, 30, 35.

26 - Joe has 7 marbles, John has 5.

27 - 6
In each group of circles, the centre number equals the average of the four surrounding numbers.

28 - 11
Split the left and right hand circles in half, vertically. The sum of the numbers in the left hand half of the left circle appears in the top left hand segment of the middle circle, and the sum of the numbers in the right hand half of the left hand circle appears in the bottom left hand segment of the middle circle. Repeat this pattern for the right hand circle.

29 - 7
In each diagram, the sum of the upper left and upper middle numbers is written in the centre box, and the sum of the upper right and upper middle numbers is written in the lower central box.

30 - 5
Taking pairs of dominoes, one from the extreme left of the row and one from the extreme right of the row, both show the same point total. Repeat this sequence, working towards the centre.

SOLUTIONS

TEST 4

1 - 6
The number at the centre of each segment equals the sum of the numbers on the outside of the opposite segment.

2 - I
Letters are arranged in each square in alphabetical order, skipping 5 letters at a time. The letter bounded by the central square carries on this sequence, but using the reverse alphabetical value.

3 - One alarm clock

4 - 23
Looking at the diagram as two columns, numbers in the left hand column increase by 5, 6, 7 etc, and numbers in the right hand column increase by 6, 7, 8 etc.

5 - 5
The numbers in the lower circles equal the numbers in corresponding segments in the upper circles multiplied by two, then subtract 3 for the left hand circle, 4 for the middle and 5 for the right hand circle.

6 - O
In each row, letters follow the alphabetic sequence, in steps of 4 letters each time for the first row, 5 letters for the second, then 6, 7 etc.

7 - 2
The diagram represents a multiplication sum : 128 x 2 = 256

8 - H
In each row of the diagram, the numerical values of the letters add up to 26.

9 - 96
Moving from left to right, numbers follow the sequence of square numbers, from 6 to 10, subtracting 4 each time. Alternatively, numbers increase by 13, 15, 17 and 19.

10 - 9
Reading each pair of numbers in a row as a 2-digit number, values increase by 6 each time.

11 - X
In each circle, start with the top left segment, and move clockwise around the other segments. The value of each letter increases by 5 for the first circle, 6 for the next, then 7, 8 and 9.

12 - 3
Reading each column as a 3-digit number, moving from left to right, the columns follow the sequence of cube numbers of 5, 6 and 7.

13 - A
Converting each letter to its numerical value, the diagram represents a subtraction sum: 247 - 54 = 193.

14 - 13
In each star, the central value equals the sum of the upper and lower digits on each star, subtracting the sum of the left and right hand digits.

15 - T
Starting on the top left, and moving in an anti-clockwise spiral towards the centre, letters advance through the alphabet by 3 letters at a time.

16 - 6
In each circle, double the numbers on the left hand side and put the result in the opposite segment on the right hand side.

17 - W
Looking at the diagram in columns, letters in the first column are written with 2 straight lines, in the second column they contain 3 straight lines, and letters in the right hand column are written with 4 straight lines.

18 - 4
Adding up the digits in each oval shape, as you move down the column this total increases by 2 each time, from 12 to 22.

19 - 1
In each circle, the number in the lower left segment equals the sum of the numbers in the top two segments, and the number in the lower right circle equals the difference between the numbers in the top two segments.

20 - C
If you convert each letter to its numerical value, and read pairs of numbers as 2-digit values, the values follow the sequence of multiples of 7.

21 - 2
Working in rows, the sum of numbers in each row follows the sequence 5, 10, 15, 20, 15, 10, 5.

22 - 9
Working from left to right, the sum of the two smaller numbers on each triangle equals the third number.

23 - G
Following lines of circles across all 3 diagrams, letters in the top line follow the alphabetic sequence, in steps of 4 letters at a time. Letters in the central line advance 5 letters, and in the bottom line, 6 letters.

24 - 6
The number in the centre of each star equals the average of the surrounding 5 numbers.

25 - F
Moving from left to right, letters move though the alphabet in sequence, advancing 12 letters, then 11, 10, 9, 8 etc.

26 - 43
In each triangle, multiply the lower two numbers together and add the upper number to give the value at the centre.

27 - D
The numerical values of the letters in each circle add up to 20.

28 - 4
Each row of the grid contains each of the 10 digits, 0 to 9, written in a random order.

29 - 6
Numbers in the segments of the lower left circle equal the sum of the corresponding numbers in the upper left and central circles. Numbers in the segments of the lower right circle equal the sum of the numbers in corresponding segments of the upper right and central circles.

30 - S
Taking the numerical value of each letter, they follow the sequence of Prime Numbers.

SOLUTIONS

TEST 5

1 - A
Working from left to right, top row then bottom row, the first grid contains 5 black dots, the second contains 7, the third 9, the fourth 11, and the fifth 13. So the sixth should contain 15 black dots.

2 - E
The sum of the separate digits on each watch increases by 2 as you move to the right.

3 - N
Starting with the A on the left hand side, move around the shape in a clockwise spiral towards the centre. Letters advance through the alphabet in steps of 4, 5 then 6, repeating this pattern all the way around.

4 - 10
The numbers on the points of the lower triangle equal the sum of the numbers on corresponding points of the upper two triangles.

5 - G
Starting with A and C, as you move clockwise, the numerical value of the next letter equals the sum of the preceding two letters.

6 - O
As you move down, letters appear in alphabetical order, skipping those letters only written with straight lines.

7 - 37
As you move down, subtract 3 from the previous number, then 5, 7, 9 and 11.

8 - 11
Taking any side of the triangle, the sum of the two corner digits is written in one of the circles on that side, and the difference is written in the other circle.

9 - W
Starting at the top left, and moving to the right, then down one row and to the left etc. in a snakes and ladders pattern, letters advance through the alphabet by 5 steps, then back 2, repeating this pattern for the rest of the diagram.

10 - S
Taking pairs of letters in the inner and outer segments of each eighth of the diagram, the numerical values always add up to 20.

11 - 90
As you move down, the numbers represent multiples of 12, subtracting 1, for the first step, adding 2 for the second, subtracting 3 for the third, adding 4 for the next, etc.

12 - 9
Reading each horizontal line as a 4-digit number, add together the top two rows to give the result in the third row, and subtract the first row number from the second to give the result in the fourth row.

13 - K
Working in columns, the alphabetical value of the three letters totals 27.

14 - S
Starting with the G, move clockwise around the circle, in steps of 3 letters, then 4, 5, 6 and 7.

15 - 3
In each row, the sum of the digits is 10.

16 - Hour hand is pointing to 2.
Multiply the hour hand value by 2 and add the minute hand value. This total is always 15.

17 - 21
Each number represents the numerical value of the vowels in the alphabet.

18 - I
As you move down, letters are written in alphabetical order, skipping any letters written with curved lines.

19 - F
Starting with the top segment of the top left square and moving clockwise around the other 3 squares, letters move through the alphabet in steps of 2, with the positions moving one place clockwise each time. Letters in the next segment of the top left square follow the same pattern, in steps of 3 letters etc.

20 - 26
Moving clockwise around the chain, numbers increase by 4, then 3, then 2, before repeating this pattern.

21 - 42
Starting in the top left and moving in a Z shape around the diagram, each number equals the sum of the previous 2 numbers.

22 - D
Starting with the bottom right letter and moving in a clockwise spiral around the diagram towards the centre, letters advance through the alphabet six letters at a time.

23 - 2
The numbers in the segments of the top left circle equal the sum of the numbers in corresponding segments of the lower two circles, and the numbers in the top right circle equal the difference between numbers in corresponding segments of the lower two circles.

24 - 1
Starting with the bottom line of the triangle and moving up, the sum of the digits in each line decreases by 5 each time, from 20 to 5.

25 - C
Converting each letter to its numerical value, and reading pairs of circles as 2-digit numbers, arranged in two vertical columns, numbers follow the sequence of multiples of 7, starting with 14 and ending with 63.

26 - 2
Numbers in the squares of the top middle figure equal the sum of the numbers in corresponding squares of the other 3 figures.

27 - 13
Starting at the top left and working down, then to the right and up, and finally to the right and down in a zig-zag shape, numbers follow the repeated sequence, subtracting 1 then adding 3 etc.

28 - 4
Working in rows from top to bottom, the sum of the digits in each row increases by 2 each time, from 20 to 30.

29 - A:15
B:38
In the first oval, all numbers are Prime Numbers.
In the second oval, all numbers are Square Numbers.

30 - 3
Working in rows, the number in the central oval equals the sum of the left and right hand numbers, divided by 3.

SOLUTIONS

TEST 6

1 - M
The 4 diagrams as a whole contain 2 sequences of letters. The first starts at the top of the top left hand diamond, and goes vertically downwards, then up to the top of the top right hand diamond and down again. Letters in this sequence are written in alphabetical order, in steps of 4 letters at a time. The second sequence starts on the left hand segment of the upper left diamond and moves in horizontal lines from left to right, top row then bottom row, with the letters written in alphabetical order in steps of 5 letters at a time.

2 - L
Moving down the first column, up the second, down the third etc. letters increase by 7 in each alternate circles.

3 - 7
In each segment of the circle, multiply the outer 2 numbers together and subtract the sum of the outer 2 numbers in the opposite segment to give the value in the inner grey segment.

4 - Q
Converting all letters to their numerical values, the middle section of each row of the diagram contains a list of letters which are common multiples of a number, given by the value of the letter in the right hand box. One letter in each row does not follow this sequence, and is put in the left hand box.

5 - S
Join pairs of letters at opposite sides of the diagram, with lines which run through the centre. The sum of the numerical values of the pairs of letters is always 25.

6 - 1
Values in the lower left table equal the sums of the values in corresponding positions of the top two tables, and values in the lower right table equal the difference in values in corresponding positions of the top two tables.

7 - N
In each star, start at the bottom and move anti-clockwise around the points. Letters follow the alphabetic sequence, in steps of 8 letters, for the left hand circle, 9 for the central one and 10 for the right hand circle.

8 - 3
In each diagram, the numerical value of the left hand letter equals the product of the upper and lower left hand numbers, and the right hand letter equals the product of the upper and lower right hand numbers. The numerical value of the central letter equals the sum of the numerical values of the left and right hand letters.

9 - 5
In each diagram, the sum of the three upper numbers equals the product of the two lower numbers.

10 - P
Start at the top of the left hand triangle and move in horizontal lines, from left to right, across all the triangles at once, top to bottom. Letters are written in sequence, skipping 2 letters, then 3, then 4, before repeating this sequence.

11 - B
In each row of the diagram, the reverse alphabetical value of the central letter equals the sum of the left and right hand digits.

12 - 12
The diagram contains two diamonds of 3x3 circles, arranged side by side, with the central 4 circles overlapping. Starting in the central left circle of each diamond, the numbers from 1 to 9 are written in lines, moving up and to the right. In the circles where the diamonds overlap, the values are added together to give the ones shown on the final diagram.

13 - 1
Add up the four outer numbers and place your answer in the centre square of the shape one place clockwise.

14 - N
Working in columns from top to bottom, left to right, letters are written in alphabetic sequence, in steps of 3 letters, then 4, then 5 etc.

15 - I
Starting with the letters in the top left square, and moving around the other squares in a clockwise spiral towards the centre, letters advance through the alphabet in steps of 4 letters at a time, with the relative positions of each letter moving 1/4 turn clockwise at each step.

16 - King of Clubs
Start at the top left of the diagram and move to the right, then down one row and to the left etc. in a snakes and ladders pattern. The value of each card increases by 5 each time, with their suit following the sequence of hearts, clubs, diamonds and spades.

17 - B
Start with the top left square and move clockwise around the others. The sum of the numerical values of the letters in each square follows the sequence 20, 25, 30 and 35.

18 - 1
Split the grid in half vertically, to give two columns, 3 squares wide. Working from top to bottom, left then right, and reading each 3 square row as a whole 3-digit number, the columns follow the sequence of square numbers, from 10 to 21.

19 - Five minutes to Ten
Start with the top left clock-face, and move around the others clockwise. The minute hand moves backwards by 15 minutes, then 20, then 25 etc, while the hour hand moves forward 2 hours, then 3, then 4 etc.

20 - G
Convert each letter to its numerical value, and read each pair of values as 2-digit numbers. In each row, the number in the centre equals the difference between the 2-digit values on the left and right.

21 -

Theatre group	Play	Opening month	Ticket price
Piecrust	Macbeth	June	£10
RSC	Othello	October	£3
CAD	Julius Caesar	March	£6

22 - 1
Taking any series of 3 numbers in a straight line in the diagram, their total is always 19.

23 - Y
Start in the top left hand corner and move anti clockwise around the perimeter of the square. Letters are written in alphabetical order, skipping 1 letter, then 2 letters, then 3 etc.

24 - A

25 - 1
Working from the top row, add the values in adjacent boxes and put this sum in the box directly below, working towards the centre. Repeat this pattern starting at the bottom row as well.

26 - The bottle is worth 50p, and the perfume is worth £9.50

27 - S
Start with the top left circle, and move in horizontal lines from left to right, top to bottom, across all 4 shapes. Letters are written in alphabetical order, in steps of 5 letters at a time.

28 - H
Start at the top left segment of the left hand circle and move clockwise, then to the middle circle and move anti-clockwise, and finally to the right hand circle and move clockwise again. Letters are written in alphabetical order, in steps of 4 letters at a time.

29 - V
Starting with the upper left hand box of the left hand diagram, and moving to the right, letters follow the alphabetical order, 5 letters at a time. A second sequence starts from the middle of this row and goes down, with letters following the alphabetic order, 6 letters at a time. Repeat this pattern for the other diagrams, using steps of 6 and 7 letters, 7 and 8 letters, and 8 and 9 letters.

30 - 5
Take each half of the dominoes separately, add together the spots shown on the first two pieces to get the third domino, then add together the spots from the second and third to get the fourth, etc. Return to 0 whenever the spot total exceeds 6.

194

SOLUTIONS

1 - E
In each row, the left hand grid is symmetrical around a vertical axis, the central grid is symmetrical about a horizontal axis, and the right hand grid is symmetrical about a diagonal axis, running bottom left to top right.

2 - A
As you move from left to right, the time shown on each watch decreases by 12 minutes, then 24, 36 and 48.

3 - 4
Working in rows, from top to bottom, the sum of the digits in each row increases by 2 each time, from 8 to 16.

4 - 9
Working clockwise around the 3 triangles, the sum of the outer digits in each triangle is written in the centre of the triangle one place clockwise.

5 - N
Starting with B and moving clockwise, letters advance through the alphabet in steps of 2, then 4, 6, 8 and 10.

6 - 72
Numbers follow the sequence of Square Numbers, from 1 to 6, multiplying each one by 2.

7 - 68
As you move down, multiply each number by 2 and subtract 4. Put another way, double the difference between each number every time.

8 - 2
The sum of the numbers along each side of the triangle is always 15.

9 - I
Convert each letter into its numerical value, and read each row as a 3-digit number. Rows follow the sequence of Square Numbers from 15 to 17.

10 - W
Starting with the top left outer segment and moving clockwise, letters advance through the alphabet in steps of 4, then 5, 6, 7 etc. The letters in the inner segments follow the same pattern, but move anti-clockwise.

11 - 16
As you move downwards, numbers increase by 3, then 2, then 1, before repeating this pattern.

12 - 7
The numbers in each row of the diagram add up to 18.

13 - G
Starting at the top left and working anti-clockwise towards the centre in a spiral, letters advance through the alphabet in steps of 8 at a time.

14 - F
Taking pairs of letters in adjacent segments, starting with the top two letters, their numerical values always add up to 10.

15 - 2
The sum of the 4 digits at the corners of the diagram is 17, as is the sum of the 4 digits in the middle of each side of the diagram.

16 - Hour hand points to 8
Starting with the top clock-face, and moving clockwise around the others, the minute hand moves forward 15 minutes, while the hour hand moves back 2 hours each time.

17 - V
Each hexagon is filled with the letter of the alphabet you find one place after the vowels.

18 - J
Adding 1 to the numerical values of each letter gives the sequence of Prime Numbers.

19 - 9
Starting with the top left square, and moving clockwise around the other 3, the sum of the digits in each square follows the sequence 20, 19, 18, 17.

20 - 71
As you move clockwise around the diagram, add the previous 2 numbers together and subtract 3 to give the next number in the chain.

21 - 9
Starting with the numbers in the top row, and following straight lines through the centre of the diagram, subtract 3 from the number and put the result in the corresponding lower circle.

22 - 2
Reading the top and bottom lines as 2-digit numbers, multiply these together to give the 3-digit result, written in the middle.

23 - 1
Numbers in the segments of the lower left circle equal the sum of the digits in corresponding segments of the upper circles. Numbers in the lower right circle equal the difference between numbers in corresponding segments of the upper circles.

24 - F
Starting with the B on the lower right of the triangle, and following the diagram round in a clockwise direction, letters move through the alphabet in steps of 5.

25 - A
In each column of the diagram, the sum of the numerical values of the letters is always 25.

26 - W
In each group of 3 squares, starting on the upper left and moving clockwise around the other 2 squares, letters follow the alphabetic sequence in steps of 6 for the left hand diagram, 7 for the upper middle, 8 for the right hand diagram and 9 for the lower one.

27 - 56
Starting at the top left and moving down, then to the right and up, in a snakes and ladders pattern, add the first two numbers together and subtract 1 to get the next in the sequence.

28 - 6
Divide the whole diagram into 4 equal quarters, each comprising of a 3x3 square. The sequence of numbers in the top left quarter is repeated in each of the other quarters, but increasing by 1 each time as you move clockwise.

29 -   A:11
        B:16
In the first oval, each number represents the numerical value of the vowels in the alphabet. In the second oval, each number represents the numerical value of letters of the alphabet written with only straight lines.

30 - 4
In each row of the diagram, the sum of the left and right hand digits, minus the central digit is always 8.

SOLUTIONS

1 - 8
Divide the circle, horizontally and vertically, to give 4 quarters. The sum of the numbers in the segments of each quarter equals 11.

2 - K
Add 6 to the numerical value of each of the larger letters, and write the letter with this value in the smaller square diagonally opposite.

3 - One carriage

4 - D
Converting each letter to its numerical value and reading each line as a 2-digit number, the numbers follow the sequence of multiples of 6, from 36 to 54.

5 - O
Starting with the left hand circle in the top row, add 4 to the numerical value of each letter and write the letter with this value in the corresponding segment of the lower left circle. Continue this pattern, adding 5 to the letter values in the central circle, and 6 in the right hand circle.

6 - A
Start at the top left of the diagram, and work down the left hand column, then along one space to the right and up the next column, in a snakes and ladders pattern, write the following repeated sequence of letters: A C P R F D U

7 - 6
Working through the diagram in rows, and reading each row as a whole number, the diagram represents a subtraction sum :
203 - 7 = 196

8 - C
Convert each letter to it's numerical value, and read horizontal lines as 2- or 3-digit numbers. Add the top 3-digit number to the 2-digit number below to give 200, repeat this pattern for the 3- and 2-digit numbers underneath.

9 - 39
Moving from left to right, add 6 to the first number to get the next one along, then 8, 10 and 12 to complete the sequence.

10 - 16
Starting with the top left number, and working down one row at a time, alternating between left and right, double the number each time. Repeat this sequence, starting with the top right number.

11 - 1
Numbers in segments of the central circle equal the difference between the sum of the numbers in corresponding segments of the left two and right two circles.

12 - 16
Working in columns, starting with the top number, add 4 to give the next value down, and add 5 to give the one under that.

13 - Z
Starting at the top left of the diagram, and moving around it in a Z shape, letters follow the alphabetic sequence, in steps of 6 letters at a time.

14 - 11
In each star, add together the top 3 numbers, and subtract the lower 2 numbers, to give the value in the centre of each star.

15 - T
Working in rows, the numerical value of the letter in the right hand column equals the sum of the numerical values of the letters in the left and central columns.

16 - T
Starting with the top left segment of each circle, and moving clockwise, letters follow the alphabetic sequence, in steps of 3 letters for the top circle, 4 letters for the left hand circle, and 5 letters for the bottom circle.

17 - 3
In each row of the diagram, add the left and right hand digits together and add 2 to give the result in the centre.

18 - 601
Starting at the top, double each number and add 7 to give the next number down.

19 - L
In each circle, the numerical value of the letter in the lower left quarter equals the sum of the numerical values of the upper 2 letters, and the numerical value of the letter in the lower right quarter equals the difference between the numerical values of the upper 2 letters.

20 - 92
Working from left to right, top to bottom, add together the first two numbers and subtract 3 to give the next value along.

21 - E
Start at the top of the diagram, and work through each row from left to right. Letters move through the alphabet, In steps of 3 letters, then 4, 5 and 6, repeating this sequence.

22 - 47
Starting at the top on the left, and working in rows across the 3 triangles, values increase by 2, then 3, then 4 etc.

23 - P
In each diagram, starting on the top left and moving clockwise in a spiral towards the centre, letters increase in value by 3 for the left hand diagram, 4 for the middle, and 5 for the right hand diagram.

24 - 9
In each star, the average of the outer 3 numbers is written in the centre of the star.

25 - V
Starting with the B in the top left, and moving left to right across the diagram in horizontal lines, letters advance through the alphabet in steps of 6 letters at a time.

26 - 21
In each triangle, add the lower 2 digits together and multiply by the upper digit to give the result in the centre.

27 - 1
In each circle, add together the numbers in the left and right hand segments, and subtract 2 to give the result in the lower segment.

28 - 1
Start at the top left and move down, then along one space to the right and up the next column, in a snakes and ladders pattern. Letters are written in alternate squares, in steps of 3 letters at a time.

29 - 1
Using the numbers in the segments of the lower two circles, the numbers in the upper left circle equal the sum of the numbers in corresponding segments of the lower 2 circles, the numbers in the upper central circle equal the difference between numbers in corresponding segments of the lower 2 circles, and the numbers in the upper right circle equal the product of the numbers in corresponding segments of the lower 2 circles.

30 - 0
Working from left to right and reading each pair of numbers as a 2-digit value, these values represent the sequence of multiples of 7, starting at 49 and finishing on 70.

SOLUTIONS

TEST ⑨

1 - K
In each square, start with the left hand segment, and move clockwise around the others. Letters are written in alphabetical order in steps of 10 for the top left square, 11 for the top right, 12 for the lower left and 13 for the lower right.

2 - 3
Work through the diagram in columns. The value in the centre of each column equals the difference between the sum of the top 2 numbers and the bottom two numbers.

3 - 2
In each slice of the circle, the difference between the outer and middle numbers is written in the inner segment of the opposite slice.

4 - J
Start on the top left of the diagram and work from top to bottom in columns, from left to right. Letters are written in alphabetic order, in a repeated sequence of steps of 5, 6 and 7.

5 - 4
Calculate the difference between adjacent numbers in the centre of each oval and put the result in the space between the two ovals in the opposite side of the diagram.

6 - 11
Numbers in the top right hand grid equal the sum of the numbers in corresponding positions in the upper and lower left hand grids, and numbers in the lower right hand grid equal the difference between numbers in corresponding positions in the upper and lower left hand grids.

7 - Q
Treat each star as 2 intersecting triangles, and start on the top or the left of each triangle in each star and move clockwise around it. Letters are written in alphabetical order in steps of 6 for the left hand star, 7 for the central one and 8 for the right hand star.

8 - 6
In each diagram, the central value equals the difference between the sums of the numbers in the left hand column and the sums of the numbers in the right hand column.

9 - 14
In each diagram, the number at the top equals the average of the four smaller numbers.

10 - 11
In each triangular group of circles, start with the longest row and add together 3 adjacent values and put this sum in the circle directly above or below the centre of the 3 values. Continue this sequence towards the apex of each triangle.

11 - 6
Calculating the sum of the 3 numbers in each row, from top to bottom, the rows follow the sequence of 11, 13, 15 etc.

12 - 5
Start with the row of 4 numbers in the centre of the diagram, and add adjacent pairs of numbers together, putting the results in the circles directly above. Repeat this pattern for the next row up. Next, calculate the difference between adjacent numbers in the middle row, putting the results in the circles directly below. Repeat this pattern for the next row down.

13 - F
Two sequences are used in these five grids, both only using the lines containing three letters. Firstly, move along the horizontal lines from top left to bottom right in steps of four, starting with the A. Secondly, move down the vertical lines in steps of six, starting with the E. Whenever two numbers cross add the numerical values together and put the solution in the middle of each cross.

14 - 6
Start with the numbers along the top right diagonal of the diagram, and add pairs of adjacent numbers together, putting the result in the square to the lower left of the original pair of numbers. Continue in this way towards the lower left hand corner.

15 - 14
Add together numbers in corresponding segments of the upper 2 squares, and put the results in the middle square. Numbers in the lower left square equal the product of the upper left and central squares, and numbers in the lower right square equal the product of the upper right and central squares.

16 - 7 (any suit)
Taking the value of aces as 1 and all other cards as per their face value. In each column of the diagram, the value of the sum of the 3 cards is always 21.

17 - K
Start with the top left hand segment of the top left hand square, and move around the other squares in a clockwise direction. Letters are written in sequence in steps of 5 letters at a time for the top left segment, 6 letters for the top right, 7 for the bottom right and 8 for the bottom left. The relative positions of the letters in each sequence move 1 segment clockwise at every step.

18 - S
Split the diagram into 3 rows, each 2 boxes high. In the top double row, letters are written in sequence, from left to right, alternating between the upper and lower row, in steps of 6 letters at a time. The middle row follows the same sequence, in steps of 7 letters at a time, as does the bottom row, in steps of 8 letters.

19 - To the 5
Start with the top left clock-face, and move around the others in a clockwise direction. The sum of the numbers pointed to by the hour and minute hand follows the sequence 14, 15, 16, 17 and 18.

20 - B
In each row, the value in the centre equals the difference between the sum of the numerical values of the pair of letters to the left and the pair of letters to the right.

21 -

Gardener	Injury	Crop	Day
Bob	Back	Roses	Wednesday
Mike	Knee	Apples	Friday
Sandra	Elbow	Potatoes	Monday

22 - K
The sum of the letters in the three adjacent circles on each side of the diagram is always 30.

23 - D
The diagram contains 3 sets of 4 letters - one set of outer corner letters, one set of inner corner letters, and one set of letters on each side of the square. The numerical values of the letters in each set add up to 40.

24 - C

25 - D
Start with the C at the centre of the diagram and follow 2 sequences of letters, both clockwise from the C, one around the upper half of the diagram, and one around the lower half. Letters in the upper half advance through the alphabet in steps of 7 letters at a time, and letters in the lower half advance in steps of 9.

26 - 7 people

27 - X
In each diagram, the central letter falls midway between the left and right hand letters, and the top and bottom letters.

28 - 4
Split the left and right hand circles into 2 halves vertically. The numerical value of the letter in the upper left segment of the central circle equals the sum of the numbers in the left half of the left hand circle, and the letter in the lower left equals the sum of the numbers in the right half of the left hand circle. Repeat this pattern for the right hand circle.

29 - I
Start on the upper left of each diagram, and move to the right, then down the last 2 boxes in the centre. Letters are written in alphabetical order, in steps of 5 for the left hand diagram, 6 for the next, then 7, then 8.

30 - 3
Starting on the left and working to the right, take pairs of dominoes and calculate the sum of the dots they are displaying. This sum follows the sequence 3, 6, 9 and 12.

SOLUTIONS

1 - K
Split the circle into 4 quarters, horizontally and vertically, with 2 segments each. Starting with the top left segment, the sum of the numerical values of the letters in the 2 segments equals 15. The sum of the next pair of segments clockwise equals 16, then 17, then 18.

2 - 9
Taking numbers in diagonally opposite squares, calculate their sum, and put the answer in the small, inner square of the upper number. Calculate their difference, and put this answer in the small, inner square of the lower number.

3 - One doughnut

4 - Q
The numerical value of the letters in each row totals 27.

5 - 1
Starting with the 3 circles in the top row, add together values in corresponding segments of the left and right hand halves of the left hand circle, and put the results in corresponding segments of the left hand half of the central circle. Repeat this pattern for the left and right hand segments of the right hand circle.
For the lower row, follow the same pattern, but calculating the differences between values in the left and right hand halves of the left and right hand circles, putting the results in the central circle.

6 - H
Start on the top left of the diagram, and move clockwise in a spiral towards the centre. Letters advance through the alphabet in steps of 5.

7 - I
Start at the top left, and work through the diagram in a Z shape, letters move through the alphabet in steps of 6, then 7, then 8 etc.

8 - 1
Taking the top 3 numbers, add them together, and write the 2-digit result in the spaces below. Repeat this pattern for the next set of numbers.

9 - 6
Working from left to right, numbers represent the reverse alphabetical values of the vowels in the alphabet.

10 - 6
Working from top to bottom, and reading each pair of boxes as a 2-digit number, add 10 to the first number to give the next one down, then add 15, then 20, and then 25 to complete the sequence.

11 - 13
As you move from left to right, the sum of the digits in each circle forms a sequence of multiples of 6, from 6 to 30.

12 - 6
Working in rows, the central value equals the difference between the left and right hand values.

13 - 18
Starting on the top left, and moving clockwise around the diagram, add the first two values together to give the next value along. Repeat this sequence.

14 - 6
For each star, add the outer numbers together and divide by 3 for the left hand, 4 for the centre, and 5 for the right hand, putting the result in the centre.

15 - O
Start on the top left and move down, then right one space and up etc in a snakes and ladders pattern. Letters advance through the alphabet in steps of 5.

16 - U
Start with the letters in the left hand circle. Subtract 3 from the numerical values of each letter, and put the letter with this value in the corresponding segments of the upper circle. Repeat this pattern, adding 3 to the numerical values of the letters, and putting the results in corresponding segments of the lower circle.

17 - N
Moving from left to right, top to bottom letters follow alphabetical order, skipping any letters written with curved lines.

18 - S
Working from top to bottom, the numerical values of the letters follow the sequence of Prime Numbers, adding 1, then 2, then 3 etc.

19 - 12
Add together numbers in corresponding segments of the upper two and lower left circles to give the values in corresponding segments of the lower right circle.

20 - 3
Starting at the top and moving down, reading each pair of boxes as a 2-digit number, numbers increasing by 3, then 6, then repeat.

21 - L
Start at the top of the diagram and work in rows, from left to right, top to bottom. Letters move through the alphabet in steps of 4, 5, 6, 7, 8, 9 and 10, before repeating this sequence.

22 - 6
In each triangle, add together the lower two digits and subtract 2 for the left hand triangle, 3 for the middle and 4 for the right hand triangle, putting the result at the apex of the triangle.

23 - 9
Add together the four outer numbers in each diagram. Divide this answer by two to get the middle number.

24 - X
Starting with the top letter in each star, and moving clockwise around the others, letters advance through the alphabet in steps of 8 for the left hand star, 9 for the central star, and 10 for the right hand star.

25 - V
Working from left to right, following the zig-zag pattern of the line, letters move through the alphabet in steps of 15 letters, then 14, then 13, etc.

26 - 12
In each triangle, the central value equals the average of the 3 values around the outside.

27 - 27
In each circle, multiply the top two numbers together, and divide by 2 for the left hand circle, 3 for the centre, and 4 for the right hand circle, putting the result in the lower segment.

28 - 2
Split the diagram horizontally and vertically into 4 quarters. A sequence of letters is written in each quarter, following the alphabetic order, 3 letters at a time, starting with the upper left quarter. Add 2 to the values of each letter to give the letters in the next quarter clockwise, then 3, then 4.

29 - 5
Take values in the top left and centre circles and put their sum in corresponding segments of the lower left circle. Take values in the middle and right hand circles, and put their difference into corresponding segments of the lower right circle.

30 - 22
Working from left to right, add numbers in the first two boxes together, and subtract 4, to give the next value along.

SOLUTIONS

TEST 11

1 - F
In each diagram, the black circles join together to make straight sided polygons. Working from left to right, top row then bottom row, the number of sides in each polygon increases by 1 each time, from 3 to 8.

2 - D
On each watch, the sum of the digits shown equals 8.

3 - F
Working in rows, from top to bottom, the sum of the numerical values of the letters in each row starts at 12, and increases by 2 as you go down each row.

4 - 32
In each triangle, add together the lower 2 digits, and multiply this by the top digit, to give the value written in the centre of the triangle.

5 - G
The numerical values of the letters in opposite segments of the circle add up to 16 each time.

6 - H
Working from top to bottom, letters are written in pairs. Take the 2-digit numerical value of the first letter and add the 2 digits together. Write the letter with this numerical value in the next space down. Continue in this way down the line.

7 - 71
As you move down, numbers increase by 3, 5, 7, 9 and 11.

8 - T
Starting in the bottom left corner of the diagram, and moving clockwise, letters follow in alphabetic order, skipping 1 letter, then 2, then 3 etc.

9 - 1
Working in columns, start with the top number, and subtract the number in the centre, to give the result in the bottom row.

10 - V
Starting with the top left outer segment and moving clockwise, alternating between the inner and outer segments, letters advance through the alphabet 5 letters at a time. Starting with the top left inner segment, follow the same pattern, using every sixth letter.

11 - 849
Working from top to bottom, add 1 to each number and multiply by 3 to give the next value down.

12 - 6
Working in rows, from top to bottom, and reading each row as a 4-digit number, rows follow the sequence of Cube Numbers, from 13 to 16.

13 - 8
Starting in the top left and working in columns, add the first two numbers together and add 1 to give the number at the bottom of each row.

14 - L
Starting with the A in the top left segment of the circle, and moving clockwise, the sequence comprises alternate letters made with only straight lines.

15 - 1
The four numbers in the corners of the square, and the four numbers in the middle of each side of the square add up to 21.

16 - The hour hand points to the 4.
The sum of the values pointed to by the hands on each clock equals 12.

17 - Y
From left to right, the numerical value of the letters represents the sequence of multiples of 5, from 5 to 25.

18 - L
Working downwards, the numerical values of the letters increase by one, two, three and four.

19 - 4
Add up numbers in corresponding segments of each square. The sum of the digits in the left hand segments equals 20, the sum of the upper segments equals 22, the right hand segments equals 24 and the lower segments equal 26.

20 - 22
There are two repeated sequences in the circle. Starting with the first segment and moving clockwise, add 1 to the first number, then 2, 3, and 4, writing the results in alternate segments. Starting with the second segment, add 3 to this number, then 4, 5 and 6, writing these results in the alternate segments left.

21 - D
Starting at the top left and moving in a Z shape around the diagram, the numerical value of the letters increases by 6, then 7, then 8 etc.

22 - 2
Reading each row as a whole number, multiply the top 2-digit number by the lower 2-digit number to give the result represented by the middle 3-digit number.

23 - 13
Starting with the top circles, multiply each value by 2 and subtract 3, writing the result in the corresponding segment of the lower circle.

24 - 6
Numbers in boxes from the second row up equal the average of the 2 numbers in the boxes directly below. Continue to the apex of the triangle.

25 - O
Working in rows, from left to right, in the top row add 3 to the numerical value of the first letter to give the next one along, then 4, then 5. In the next row, add 5 to the first letter, then 6, then 7. In the third row, start by adding 7, then 8, then 9, and in the bottom row, add 9, then 10, then 11.

26 - O
In each group of 3 boxes, the numerical value in the lower box equals the average of the numerical values of the letters in the top 2 boxes.

27 - 2
Reading each line of the diagram as a 3-digit number, add the top and middle lines together to give the result on the bottom line.

28 - Y
Split the diagram into equal quarters of 3x3 squares. In each quarter, move around the spaces in a clockwise spiral towards the centre, starting on the top left. Letters follow the alphabetic sequence, In steps of 2 letters, then 3, then 4 etc.

29 -   1:Q
            2:D
The first oval contains letters with even numerical values, and the second oval contains letters with odd numerical values (which are also prime numbers).

30 - 1
In each row, add the left and right hand numbers together and subtract 2 to give the number in the centre of the row.

SOLUTIONS

1 - B
In each square, the sum of the numerical values of the top and bottom letters equals the sum of the left and right hand letters.

2 - 11
Working through the diagram in columns, the value at the bottom of each column equals the sum of the top 2 numbers, minus the sum of the next 2 numbers.

3 - F
Add together the numerical values of the letters which appear in the outer segments, and put the letter with this value in the inner segment, one place clockwise.

4 - Z
In each row, multiply the numerical values of the left and right hand letters, putting the result in the centre.

5 - Y
Start on the left hand of the diagram, and move clockwise. Letters are written in alphabetical order, in steps of 10 letters at a time.

6 - 8
In each grid, working in columns, add the top and bottom numbers together, and put this sum in the centre square in the grid underneath the original (for the top grids), or the grid above (for the lower grids).

7 - 5
In each star, the value at the centre equals the difference between the sum of the top 3 numbers and the sum of the bottom 3 numbers.

8 - F
In each diagram, convert each letter to its numerical value, and read the top and bottom pairs of letters as complete 2-digit values. Multiply these values together to give the 3-digit result written in the centre spaces.

9 - 4
In each diagram, read the upper and lower pairs of numbers as 2-digit values and add these together to give the result written at the top.

10 - X
In each triangular shape, start on the extreme left and move in a clockwise spiral towards the centre. Letters are written in alphabetical order, in steps of 6 letters for the left hand shape, 7 letters for the centre, and 8 letters for the right hand shape.

11 - 4
Working in rows, add the left and right hand values together and subtract 3 to give the number in the centre of each row.

12 - B
Start on the left of the diagram, and work in columns, top to bottom, from left to right. Letters are written in sequence, in steps of 2, then 4, then 6, then 8, before repeating this pattern.

13 - 4
Add together the four outer numbers of each grid. This answer is the central number of the grid one place further clockwise.

14 - 10
Working in columns, the sum of the numbers in each column equals 23.

15 - 5
Add together numbers in corresponding segments of the outer four squares. The answer is placed in the diagonally opposite segment of the middle square.

16 - Jack of Spades
There are 2 sequences in the grid - one determining the value of the card, and one determining the suit of the card. Starting on the top left and moving right, then down one row and to the left, then down the final row and to the right, cards are arranged in order, with their value increasing by 4 each time. To calculate the suit of each card, start on the top left and move down, then right one row and move up etc. cards are arranged in the order Hearts, Clubs, Diamonds, Spades.

17 - Y
Work in rows, across the 4 squares as a whole. Start at the top left and move to the right, then down one row and to the left etc in a snakes and ladders pattern. Letters advance through the alphabet in steps of 5 letters at a time.

18 - 6
Split the diagram into 2 halves vertically, each 3 columns wide. Numbers in the left hand half follow the sequence of cubed numbers, from 64 to 729, and numbers in the right hand half follow the sequence of squared numbers, from 121 to 256.

19 - To the 6
Starting with the top left clock-face and working clockwise around the others, the sum of the numbers pointed to by the 2 hands starts at 3 and increases by 2 each time.

20 - W
In each row, take the reverse alphabetical value of the left hand letter and the alphabetical value of the right hand letter and calculate the difference, putting this result in the central square.

21 -

Child	Mother	Costume	Age
Andrew	Paula	Carrot	8
Daisy	Jane	T.V.	7
Lily	Mary	Martian	9

22 - F
Taking pairs of letters at opposite sides of the diagram, the sum of their numerical values equals 21 each time.

23 - T
Start at the top left, and move clockwise around the square. Letters follow the alphabetical order, in steps of 4 letters, then 5, 6, 7, 8, 9 and 10, before repeating this sequence.

24 - C

25 - O
Start at the centre letter, and move around the upper triangle in a clockwise direction. Letters follow the alphabetical order in steps of 9 letters at a time. Repeat the same pattern, moving clockwise around the lower triangle, with the letters written in steps of 7 letters at a time.

26 - Thirty men

27 - 2
In each diagram, the central value equals the sum of the left and right hand digits, minus the sum of the upper and lower digits.

28 - J
Start on the upper left hand segment of the left hand circle and move anti-clockwise around it. Then move to the upper left of the central circle and move clockwise, then on to the right hand circle, and again move anti-clockwise. Letters are written in sequence along this path, in steps of 3 letters, then 4, 5 and 6, before repeating this sequence.

29 - 4
In each shape, use the left and right hand numbers as a source. The upper central number equals the sum of the left and right hand numbers, the middle central number equals the product of the left and right hand numbers, and the lower central number equals the difference between the left and right hand numbers.

30 - 3
As you move from left to right, the spot total on each domino increases by 3 then decreases by 1 alternately.

SOLUTIONS

TEST 13

1 - B
Working in rows, left to right, top row then bottom, one black circle is added each time, with the positions of the circles moving 1/4 turn clockwise each time.

2 - E
Taking the hour and minute values on each watch separately, as you move to the right the hour value increases by 1, 2, 3 and 4, and the minute value decreases by 11, 22, 33 and 44.

3 - 5
Working in rows, in each row the central number is equal to the difference between the sum of the even numbers in the row and the sum of the odd numbers in the row.

4 - V
Starting with the top left triangle, and moving clockwise around the other 2, letters advance through the alphabet in steps of 4, 5 and 6, with their relative positions moving 1 place clockwise around each triangle.

5 - 196
Starting with the top left segment, and moving clockwise around the circle, numbers follow the sequence of square numbers, from 121 to 256.

6 - M
As you move down the line of letters, alphabetical values increase by 7, then 4, then 7 etc.

7 - 57
As you work down the column, numbers increase by 5, 7, 9, 11 and 13.

8 - 1
Splitting the diagram into 3 smaller triangles, with 3 circles each, the sum of the numbers in each smaller triangle is always 21.

9 - D
Starting on the top left, and moving to the right, then down one row and to the left etc. in a snakes and ladders pattern, letters advance through the alphabet in steps of 5, then 2, then 5 etc.

10 - N
Take pairs of letters, one from an outer segment and one from the inner segment in the opposite position. The sum of the numerical values of these letters is always 20.

11 - 69
Starting at the top and working down, numbers increase by 2, 4, 8, 16 and 32.

12 - 5
Working in columns, the sum of the numbers in each column equals 18.

13 - C
In each row, the numerical value of the central letter equals the sum of the numerical values of the left and right hand letters.

14 - B
Starting with the top left segment and moving clockwise, letters advance through the alphabet in steps of 4, then 5, then 6 etc.

15 - 16
Starting on the top left, and moving clockwise in a spiral towards the centre, numbers increase by 7, then decrease by 2. Repeat this pattern all the way around.

16 - Minute hand pointing to 6
Starting with the top clock-face and moving clockwise around the others, the hour hand moves forward by 1 hour, then 2, then 3, while the minute hand moves forward 10 minutes, then 20, then 30.

17 - 10
Working from left to right numbers follow the sequence of Prime Numbers, subtracting 1 each time.

18 - J
Working from top to bottom, letters appear in alphabetical order, skipping any letters written with only straight lines.

19 - Q
Starting with the top left square, and moving clockwise around the other squares, the numerical values of each letter increase by 2, with their relative positions in each square rotating 1 place clockwise at each turn.

20 - 24
Working clockwise around the diagram, add the first two numbers together and subtract 3 to give the next number along.

21 - G
Starting with the letters in the top row, and following straight lines through the middle circle, subtract the numerical value of the middle letter (G) and write the letter with the corresponding numerical value in the lower circle.

22 - Y
Starting with the bottom left letter and moving in a clockwise spiral towards the centre, letters advance through the alphabet in steps of 4, 5, 6 etc.

23 - 3
In each circle, the sum of the numbers in the left hand half of the circle equals double that of the numbers in the right hand half of the circle.

24 - E
Starting with the bottom row and moving up, one row at a time, the sum of the numerical values of the letters starts at 26 for the bottom row, then 24, 22 and 20 as you move up.

25 - X
Starting with the bottom right hand corner, and moving in a clockwise spiral towards the centre, letters advance through the alphabet, skipping 4 letters at a time.

26 - 11
Starting with the diagram in the top left, and moving to the right, ending up with the bottom diagram, average the values in the top two boxes and put the result in the lower box, adding 1 for the first diagram, 2 for the next, then 3, then 4.

27 - 9
Working in rows, top to bottom, reading each row as a 3-digit number, rows follow the sequence of Square Numbers from 11 to 13.

28 - P
Starting in the top left corner and moving clockwise in a spiral towards the centre, letters follow the alphabetic sequence, skipping 5 letters at a time, written in alternate squares of the diagram.

29 - A: 42
     B: 52
In the first oval, all numbers are multiples of 4 and of 12.
In the second oval, all numbers are multiples of 3 and of 6.

30 - 5
In each row, add together the left and right hand numbers, then add 2 to give the central value.

201

SOLUTIONS

TEST 14

1 - 156
Start with 1 and move clockwise, doubling the difference between the numbers at each step (5, 10, 20, 40 and 80).

2 - 1
In every row of the diagram, if you subtract the odd numbers from the even number, you always get 10.

3 - To the 4
The sum of the numbers pointed to by the hour and minute hands is always 11.

4 - C
The sum of the numerical values of pairs of letters, opposite each other in the diagram, is always 20 (the numerical value of the central letter).

5 - 5
The values in the segments of the upper middle circle equal the sum of the values in corresponding segments of the upper left and right hand circles, and the values in the segments of the lower middle circle equal the difference between values in corresponding segments of the lower left and right hand circles.

6 - M
In each diagram, start with the upper left box, and move anti-clockwise around the others. Letters advance through the alphabet in steps of 7 for the upper left diagram, 8 for the middle, then 9, then 10.

7 - B
Starting at the top and working down, letters move through the alphabet in steps of 8 letters, then 9, then 10 etc.

8 - 37
As you move down the diagram, double the difference between the numbers at each step (1, 2, 4, 8 and 16).

9 - K
Split the diagram in half horizontally and vertically. Start in the top left square of each quarter, and move clockwise around the other squares in the quarter. In each quarter, letters advance through the alphabet in steps of 2 for the upper left quarter, 3 for the upper right, 4 for the lower right and 5 for the lower left.

10 - U
Start with the D on the outer left of the diagram, and move clockwise around the outer segments, then start on the N anti-clockwise around the inner segments. Letters advance through the alphabet in steps of 3, then 4, 5, and 6, repeating this sequence.

11 - J
In each circle, the reverse alphabetical value of the lower letter equals the sum of the alphabetical values of the top 2 letters.

12 - B
Start at the top left and move down the left hand column, then move one place to the right and up the next column etc. in a snakes and ladders pattern. Letters are written in alternate spaces, in steps of 7 letters at a time.

13 - 6
In each row of the diagram, the numerical value of the middle letter equals the sum of the left and right hand numbers, subtracting 3.

14 - 17
In each star, the number in the centre equals the difference between the sum of the even numbers and the sum of the odd numbers around the points of the star.

15 - R
The sum of the numerical values of letters in opposite segments of the circle is always 22.

16 - 26
Starting on the top left and moving to the right, then down one row and to the left, then down to the bottom row and to the right, numbers alternately add 8 then subtract 3.

17 - A
In each diagram, there are 2 lines of black dots, joining two sides together. The sides joined by the dots moves 1/4 turn clockwise as you move from left to right.

18 - H
Starting at the top and moving down, the sum of the numerical values of the letters in each oval follows the sequence 20, 22, 24 etc.

19 - 5
Take pairs of numbers at opposite ends of the diagram. Their total is always 10.

20 - M
Start with the top left square, and move clockwise around the others. The sum of the numerical values of the letters in each square equals 20 for the top left, 25 for the top right, 30 for the bottom right and 35 for the bottom left.

21 - D
Start on the bottom left and move up to the top, then to the right one space and down to the bottom. Letters follow the alphabetic sequence alternately in steps of 6, then 8. Starting on the bottom right and moving up to the top, then left one space and down to the bottom, letters in this half follow the same pattern.

22 - 11
In each triangle, the central value equals the sum of the 2 even numbers from the outside corners of the triangle minus the odd number.

23 - N
Starting at the top left hand of every diagram, move around the outer circles in an anti-clockwise direction. Letters are written in alphabetic sequence, in steps given by the numerical value of the central letter.

24 - 5
Start at the top of each triangle and move clockwise around its points. Add the first two numbers together and subtract 2 to give the next value round.

25 - E
Starting on the left, and moving to the right, letters are written in alphabetical order, moving forward 8 places, then back 2, then forward 7 places and back 3. Repeat this sequence to the end of the line. Put another way, the top and bottom rows (from left to right) move 10 places, the middle row moves 5 places.

26 - 8
In each triangle, multiply the lower 2 numbers together and subtract the upper number to give the value in the centre.

27 - 10
For each circle, add the left and right hand numbers together and put this total in the lower segment of the next circle, moving to the right and then back the start.

28 - D
Start with the watch on the left and move to the right. The time on the watches increases by 2 hours 3 minutes, then decreases by 1 hour 16 minutes, alternately.

29 - W
Start with A on the left hand side, and move in a clockwise spiral around the diagram. Letters advance through the alphabet in steps of 6.

30 - Z
Starting on the left and moving right, letters are written in alphabetical order, using every other letter written with only straight lines.

202

SOLUTIONS

TEST 15

1 - 7
In each square, multiply the top and bottom numbers together to give a 2-digit result, and put the letters with the numerical values of each digit in the left and right hand spaces.

2 - M
In each column, add up each number and put the letter with this sum in the bottom circle.

3 - I
Start with the outer top left segment, and move around the circle clockwise, then move in to the middle segments and move anticlockwise. Following this path, letters advance through the alphabet in steps of 7 letters at a time.

4 - 0
In each row, the left hand number equals the total of the even valued letters in the middle box, and the right hand number equals the total of the odd valued letters in the middle box.

5 - 9
Multiply numbers in adjacent circles together, then subtract the original numbers, to give the value in the space in-between.

6 - S
In each grid, start in the top left and move down, then right one space and up etc. in a snakes and ladders pattern. Letters advance through the alphabet in steps of 5 for the top left grid, 6 for the top right, 7 for the bottom left and 8 for the bottom right.

7 - 1
In each star, calculate the difference between the 2 left hand and 2 right hand numbers. The value at the top of each star equals the product of these differences, and the value at the bottom of each star equals the difference between these 2 differences.

8 - F
In each shape, start at the bottom left and move up, then diagonally down to the right, and finally up the right hand column, in an N shape. Letters move through the alphabet in steps of 4, 5, 6, 7, 8, and 9.

9 - 6
In each figure, calculate the difference between the upper and lower left hand numbers, and the upper and lower right hand numbers and multiply these differences together to give the value at the top.

10 - 43
In each triangle shape, start at the left hand side of the longest row and move to the right, then on the next row and to the left, and finally to the third row. Add together the first two numbers and subtract 1 to give the next value around.

11 - 2
Working from top to bottom, and reading each row as a 3-digit number, rows are arranged in order of the Square Numbers, from 11 to 15, with the digits reversed in each case.

12 - 6
Work through the diagram in horizontal rows. The sum of the numbers in each row is always 23.

13 - 6
Take values in corresponding positions of the outer 4 shapes, and put the results in the central shape, rotating the position of this result by 1/4 turn each time.

14 - Z
Start at the top, and work left to right in rows, top to bottom. Letters advance through the alphabet in steps of 10, 11, 12, 13 etc.

15 - 9
Calculate the sum of the numbers in corresponding positions of the outer 4 squares, subtract 5 from this result, and put it in the corresponding position of the middle square, 1/4 turn anticlockwise from the original.

16 - 3 of Spades
Divide the diagram in half, vertically. In each half, start at the top left card and move to the right, then down one row and to the left, and finally to the right, in a snakes and ladders pattern. The value of the cards in the left hand half increase alternately by 3 and 4, and the value of the cards in the right hand half increase alternately by 4 and 5. To calculate the suit of each card, start at the top left of the whole diagram and move down, then to the right one space and upwards etc. in a snakes and ladders pattern. Suits are written in order, following this path, starting with Hearts, then Clubs, Diamonds and Spades.

17 - I
Start in the bottom left hand corner of the diagram and, moving around the whole diagram, work in a clockwise direction, around the outer squares. Letters are written in alphabetical order, in steps of 7 letters at a time. For the single square still remaining in each group of 4, add the numerical values of the other 3 letters in the square together to give a 2-digit number, and add these separate digits together, and put the letter with this numerical value in the central square.

18 - M
Start with the top row, second square from the right, and move down and to the right in diagonal lines, advancing across the diagram to the left. Letters are written in alphabetical order, in steps of 5 at a time.

19 - To the 2
Starting with the top left clock-face and moving clockwise around the others, the minute hand moves back 2 places, then 4, 6 and 8, while the hour hand moves forward 2 places, then 4, 6 and 8.

20 - C
In each row, calculate the difference between the 2 numbers in the left hand column, and the 2 numbers in the right hand column. Multiply these differences together to give the numerical value of the letter in the centre.

21 -

Contestant	Position	Style	Prize
Marc	3rd	French	Clock
Jane	2nd	Italian	Pots+pans
Sue	1st	Chinese	Hamper

22 - B
Start at the top, and move diagonally down and to the right. Letters advance through the alphabet in steps of 5 then 6. Continue this pattern, starting with the next circle down on the left etc.

23 - S
Start with the letter in the top left, and move clockwise around the square. The numerical value of the letters follows the sequence of prime numbers, from 2 to 19.

24 - B

25 - A
Starting in the top left, and moving in rows, left to right, top to bottom, letters advance through the alphabet in steps of 6, 7 and 8.

26 - 5 years

27 - O
Start on the left of the middle row of letters, and move to the right, across all four diagrams. Letters advance through the alphabet in steps of 2, 3, 4... etc. In each separate diagram, letters also follow a sequence, moving from top to bottom, through the centre, with the value of the letters increasing by 2 each time for the left hand diagram, then 3, then 4, then 5 for the right hand diagram.

28 - 4
Split the left and right hand circles in half vertically. The letter with the numerical value of the sum of the digits in the left half of the left hand circle is placed in the top left segment of the central circle, and the letter with the numerical value of the sum of the digits in the right half of the left hand circle is placed in the top right segment of the central circle. Repeat this formula for the 2 halves of the right hand circle, putting the resulting letters in the lower segments of the central circle.

29 - J
Start on the top left of the left hand diagram, and move in horizontal lines, from left to right, top to bottom, across all 4 diagrams as a whole. Letters advance through the alphabet in steps of 7, then back 2, repeating this sequence all the way around.

30 - 6
Start on the left and move to the right, taking pairs of dominoes. The difference between the spot total of the two dominoes in each pair follows the sequence 4, 6, 8, 10.

203

SOLUTIONS

TEST 16

1 - Y
Starting with the G and moving clockwise, letters advance through the alphabet in steps of 3 letters, then 4, then 5 etc.

2 - V
Starting on the top left of each outer square, and moving clockwise around the corners of the squares, letters advance through the alphabet in steps of 4 for the upper left square, 5 for the upper right, 6 for the lower right and 7 for the lower left. Additionally, the letters bounded by the central square take the reverse alphabetical value of the original letter.

3 - One anchor

4 - 6
Working from top to bottom, reading each pair of numbers as a 2-digit value, values represent the reverse alphabetical value of letters of the alphabet, starting with A, written with 3 straight lines only.

5 - 1
Starting with the circle on the top left, and moving to the right, top row then bottom row, the sum of the numbers in each circle follows the sequence 12, 15, 18, 21 etc.

6 - B
Start on the top left, and work through the diagram in columns, from left to right. The sum of the numerical values of the letters in each column starts at 20, then increases by 1 as you move one column to the right.

7 - S
Starting at the top left of the diagram, and moving in a Z shape, letters advance through the alphabet in steps of 5.

8 - 4
Split the whole diagram in half, horizontally, to give two groups of 5 octagons. In each group, the central number in the top row equals the sum of the surrounding 4 numbers.

9 - 110
Starting on the left and moving right, double each number and add 2 to give the next number along.

10 - 4
Reading each pair of numbers as 2-digit values, the sum of the 4 numbers is given in the top space in the diagram.

11 - 12
In each circle, the number in the lower segment equals twice the difference between the numbers in the left and right hand segments.

12 - 5
Working through the diagram in rows, add the left and central numbers together and subtract 2 to give the right hand value.

13 - 2
Reading each row as a 3- or 2-digit number, subtract the central 2-digit value from the upper 3-digit value, to give the 3-digit result on the lower row.

14 - Y
Start with the top point of each star, and move clockwise around the other points. Letters advance through the alphabet in steps of 5 for the left hand star, 6 for the central star, and 7 for the right hand star.

15 - Q
Working in columns, add the numerical value of the top and middle letters together to give the numerical value of the lower letter.

16 - 10
Starting with the left hand circle, add 4 to each number and rotate their positions 1 place clockwise to give the values in the upper right hand circle, then add 5 to each of these values and rotate their positions 1 place clockwise to give the values in the lower right hand circle.

17 - 30
Working in columns, add the top and middle values to give the bottom value.

18 - 281
Working from top to bottom, numbers follow the sequence of multiples of 14, from 112 to 182, with each value being written back to front.

19 - M
Start with the letters in the top left circle, and move around the other circles in a clockwise direction. Letters advance through the alphabet 6 letters at a time, with the relative positions of each letter moving one place clockwise each time.

20 - 20
Working from top to bottom, the sum of the numbers in each row is put in the left hand box on the row below, and the difference between the two numbers in each row is put in the right hand box on the row below.

21 - 22
On each row of the diagram, the value in the centre of each row equals the sum of the other numbers in the row, subtracting 2.

22 - Y
Start at the top to the left hand triangle, and work across the whole diagram in horizontal lines from left to right, top to bottom. Letters are written in alphabetic sequence, skipping 3 letters each time.

23 - 3
In each diagram, the sum of the top two and middle digits equals the sum of the lower 2 digits.

24 - Z
In each star, start with the letter in the lower left hand point, and move around the other points in a clockwise direction. Letters advance through the alphabet in steps of 6 for the left hand star, 7 for the one in the centre, and 8 for the right hand star.

25 - N
Start on the left, and move to the right. Letters advance through the alphabet in steps of 2, then 3, then 4 etc.

26 - T
In each triangle, start with the bottom left letter, and move clockwise around the other points. Letters advance through the alphabet in steps given by the numerical value of the letter at the centre of the triangle.

27 - 6
In each circle, add together the left and right hand digits, and add 3 to give the value of the lower digit.

28 - 4
Splitting the diagram in half horizontally and vertically, each quarter contains the alphabet written in sequence, with the relative position of this sequence rotating 1/4 turn anti-clockwise as you move clockwise around the quarters.

29 - 1
Start with the top left circle, and move around the others in a W shape. The sum of the numbers in each circle follows the sequence of 10, 12, 14, 16 and 18.

30 - Q
Start on the left and work to the right. There are two alternating sequences of letters - one starts with A and moves through the alphabet 5 letters at a time. The other starts on H and moves through the alphabet 3 letters at a time.

SOLUTIONS

TEST 17

1 - A
Working in rows, if you superimpose the pattern of spots in the left and right hand grids you get the pattern in the central grid.

2 - B
As you move from left to right, add 1 to the value of each digit on the watch, and rotate the digits one place to the left.

3 - O
Working in rows, add up the digits in each row and put the letter with this numerical value in the centre of the row.

4 - 13
In each triangle, add up the lower 3 digits and divide by 3 to give the value at the apex of the triangle.

5 - 98
Starting with the lowest number and moving clockwise, add the separate digits of the first number together and add this to the original number, writing the result in the next segment along.

6 - 33
Add the first two numbers together and then subtract 4 to give the next number along.

7 - B
Working from top to bottom, replace each letter with its numerical value and read each pair of numbers as a 2-digit number. Numbers follow the sequence of multiples of 9, from 27 to 72.

8 - V
Start at the top, and work through the triangle in horizontal rows, from top to bottom, left to right. Letters move through the alphabet 5 letters at a time.

9 - 13
Working in rows, from left to right, double the left hand number to get the middle number, and add 3 to this to get the right hand number.

10 - Y
Start with the outer segment in the top left, and move anti-clockwise. Letters advance through the alphabet in steps of 6, then 7, then 8. Continue around the outer segments of the diagram, then move in an anti-clockwise direction around the inner segments.

11 - R
Working from top to bottom, letters move through the alphabet in steps of 2, then 3, then 2 etc.

12 - 2
Split the diagram into two halves vertically, consisting of 2 columns of 2 squares each, and read each 2 adjoining squares as a complete 2-digit number. Numbers increase by 7 each time.

13 - 11
Working through the diagram in columns, add 4 to the top number to give the middle one, and add 6 to this number to give the lowest one.

14 - I
Starting with the top two segments, the sum of the numerical values of letters in adjoining pairs of segments equals 20.

15 - 4
Working in rows, starting with the central row, add the left and right hand digits together and put the result in the central space. Repeat for the upper and lower rows, but put the result in the opposite central space.

16 - To the 4
Starting with the top clock-face and moving clockwise around the others, the minute hand points to the value 3 less than that pointed to by the hour hand. Repeat for the other clock-faces, subtracting 4, 5 and 6 from the hour hand values.

17 - 25
Starting on the left, halve the first number and add it to the second number to give the next one along. Repeat this sequence all the way to the right.

18 - 6
As you move down, numbers represent the reverse alphabetical values of the 5 vowels.

19 - V
Start with the top segment of the top left square, and move directly downwards. Each group of 4 letters follows the alphabetic sequence, in steps of 5 letters at a time. Taking other straight lines vertically and horizontally through the diagram, letters follow the same pattern.

20 - 93
Starting with the top segment, and moving clockwise, add the numbers in the first two segments together and subtract 7 to give the next number around.

21 - 6
Starting with the numbers in the top row, left to right, multiply each one by 2 and write the results in the lower row, from right to left.

22 - U
Starting with the top left letter, and moving clockwise around the others, letters advance through the alphabet in steps given by the numerical value of the central letter (6).

23 - 8
Starting with the numbers in the top two circles, add numbers in corresponding left hand segments of each circle, and put these values in the corresponding left hand segments of the lower left circle. Put the difference between segments in the right hand halves of the two top circles in the right hand half of the lower left circle. Repeat this pattern for the lower right circle, but putting the difference between numbers in the left hand half of the top two circles in the left hand half of the lower right circle, and the sum of the right hand half of the top two circles in the right hand half of the lower right circle.

24 - 33
Starting with numbers on the bottom row, add numbers in adjacent boxes together, and put the result in the box directly above. Continue in this way, up the pyramid.

25 - 9
Reading each row as a 4-digit number, from top to bottom, rows follow the sequence of Cube Numbers from 16 to 19.

26 - F
In each group of 3 boxes, calculate the difference in numerical values between the top two letters, and add 1 to give the value of the letter in the lower box.

27 - U
Starting in the top left of the diagram, and working in columns, from top to bottom, letters follow the alphabetical sequence, advancing 2 letters, then 4, then 6, then 8 etc.

28 - 1
Split the diagram into 3 columns, each 2 spaces wide, and read each double space as a 2-digit number. Starting at the top of each column, add the 2 separate digits together, then add this to the whole 2-digit number, to give the result, written in the spaces underneath.

29 - A:18
B:72
In the first oval, all numbers are divisible by 8, and in the second, they are all divisible by 7.

30 - 5
Working through the diagram in rows, find the difference between the left and right hand values, then add 2 to give the value in the central space.

SOLUTIONS

TEST 18

1 - 2
In each square, multiply the top and bottom numbers together to give a 2-digit result, and write this result in the left and right hand spaces.

2 - 1
Working through the diagram in rows, the central value equals the sum of the other numbers in the row.

3 - 8
Multiply the 2 numbers in the outer segments together and add 1 to give the value in the inner segment opposite.

4 - 5
In each row, add together the numerical values of the 3 central letters to give a 2-digit sum, and put this 2-digit sum in the left and right hand boxes at the end of the rows.

5 - B
Start at the top of the diagram, and move clockwise. Letters appear in alphabetical order, in steps of 10 letters at a time.

6 - 3
Split each grid into 2 halves, vertically, leaving 2 columns, each 2 squares wide. Start with the top left pair and move down, then to the top right pair, and down again. Reading each pair of digits as 2-digit values, the 2-digit values increase by 11, 12, 13, 14 and 15.

7 - 11
In each star, the number in the centre equals the difference between the sum of the numbers in the upwards triangle and the sum of the numbers in the downward triangle.

8 - H
In each diagram, add the numerical value of the upper right and left letters to the lower right and left letters, to give the letters in the centre of the columns. Calculate the difference between these middle letters to give the value of the letter right at the centre.

9 - 2
In each diagram, multiply the numbers shown on the arms together and add the number at the very top to give a 2-digit result, written in the lower 2 spaces.

10 - F
Start in the top left of the diagram and move to the right, then down one row and to the left, and finally to the right again. Letters are written in alphabetical order, in steps of 5 letters at a time.

11 - P
Working in rows, add the value of each letter to the numbers either side. The total in each row is 27.

12 - C
Start with the A in the bottom left corner, and move in a clockwise spiral around the diagram towards the centre. Letters are written in alphabetic order, in steps of 6 letters at a time.

13 - 0
Use the top two diagrams as a source. Numbers in corresponding positions in the lower left diagram equal the sums of the numbers in the top two diagrams, numbers in the central diagram equal their product, and numbers in the lower right diagram equal their difference.

14 - 4
From left to right, column totals increase by 4.

15 - P
Start with the top left grid and move around the others in a clockwise spiral towards the centre. Letters follow alphabetic sequences, skipping 1, 2, 3 and 4 letters at a time, with their relative positions in each grid rotating 1/4 turn clockwise each time.

16 - Nine of Clubs
In each column of the diagram, add the top and bottom card values together and subtract 2 to give the value of the central card.

17 - 9
Using the top two grids as a source, numbers in the lower left grid equal the sums of numbers in corresponding positions of the top two grids, subtracting 1 each time, and numbers in the lower right grid equal the differences between numbers in corresponding positions of the top two grids, adding 1 each time.

18 - 19
Divide the diagram in half, horizontally and vertically, to give 4 squares, each 3x3. In each square, add up the 4 outer numbers, and put the result in the space in the centre.

19 - To the 5
Start with the top left clock-face and move clockwise around the others. The sum of the numbers pointed to by the hour and minute hand follows the sequence 3, 6, 9, 12 and 15.

20 - T
In each row, add together the numerical values of the pairs of letters to the left and right, then calculate their difference, putting the letter with this numerical value in the centre space.

21 -

Reader	Book type	Hero	Book length
Anne	Romance	Max Morris	120 pgs
Beryl	Thriller	Lucy Carr	250 pgs
Frank	Biography	Pete Shear	400 pgs

22 - K
Start on the left hand side, and move clockwise around the diagram. Letters advance through the alphabet 9 letters at a time.

23 - 9
Take any group of 5 numbers along the side of the square, and their total is always 25.

24 - B

25 - M
Working in rows, from top to bottom, the sum of the numerical values of the letters follows the sequence 16, 18, 20, 22, 24.

26 - Mark gets £50, Patrick gets £150 and Peter gets £300.

27 - 29
In each diagram, add up the 4 outer numbers then add 2 for the left hand group, 4 for the next, then 6, then 8, and put this result in the central circle.

28 - 1
Calculate the sums of the numbers in the left and right hand circles, to give 2-digit answers. Write the left hand answer in the top 2 segments of the central circle, and put the right hand answer in the bottom 2 segments of the central circle.

29 - 56
In each diagram, multiply the left hand number by the upper central number to give the central number one line down, and multiply the right hand number by the upper central number to give the lower central number.

30 - 4
Start on the left and move to the right, taking pairs of dominoes. The sum of each pair of dominoes follows the sequence 5, 10, 15 and 20.

206

SOLUTIONS

1 - B
In each row, the left hand grid contains one line of black dots, the central one contains 2 lines and the right hand one contains 3 lines.

2 - A
On each watch, the time shown contains two digits that are the same.

3 - Z
Start on the top left of the diagram, and move from left to right, top row to bottom row. Letters advance through the alphabet in steps of 6, 7 then 8, before repeating this pattern.

4 - Q
Starting on the top left, and moving around the whole diagram in an anti-clockwise direction, outside then inside, letters advance through the alphabet 5 letters at a time.

5 - 3
Split the circle in half vertically, and take pairs of digits from corresponding segments of the left and right hand halves of the circle. Reading these pairs of digits as 2-digit numbers, these numbers follow the sequence of multiples of 9, from 45 to 63.

6 - 5
As you go down, alternately subtract 8 to give the next number, then divide by 2. Repeat this pattern.

7 - 89
Working from top to bottom, numbers represent the sequence of Square Numbers, from 144 to 289, with the first digit left out.

8 - G
Start at the top of the triangle and move anti-clockwise around it. Letters move through the alphabet in steps of 3, 4, 5, 6 etc.

9 - 8
In each row, the middle value equals the sum of the left and right hand values, adding 2 for the top row, 4 for the middle row, and 6 for the bottom row.

10 - D
Start with the H in the top left segment, and move clockwise around the shape, alternating between outer segment then inner segment. Letters advance through the alphabet 6 letters at a time.

11 - 38
Starting at the top, add 4 to the first number to get the second, then add 5, 6, 7 etc.

12 - 0
Working through the diagram in rows, the right hand value equals the sum of any odd numbers in the rest of the row.

13 - 3
The sum of the numbers in each column of the diagram is always 21.

14 - L
Starting with H and moving anti-clockwise, letters advance through the alphabet in steps of 10, then 8, then 6 etc.

15 - 7
Add the number at each corner of the diagram to its 2 adjacent numbers. The total is always 15.

16 - To the 8
Start with the top clock-face and move clockwise around the others. The sum of the numbers pointed to by the 2 hands follows the sequence 5, 10, 15, 20.

17 - 17
As you move to the right, double the first number to give the next one, then subtract 5. Repeat this sequence.

18 - J
As you move down, add the number of straight lines in the first letter to the numerical value of that letter to give the next one down.

19 - F
Start with the A in the top left hand segment, and move in straight vertical lines, from top to bottom, left to right. Letters follow the alphabetic sequence, skipping 1 letter, then 2, then 3 etc.

20 - 518
As you move clockwise, subtract 3 from the first number and multiply by 2 to give the next one round.

21 - E
Start at the top left, and move around the diagram in a Z shape. The numerical value of the letters increases alternately by 6, then 3.

22 - E
Convert each letter to its numerical value, and split the diagram into rows, reading each row as a 2- or 3-digit value. The value represented by the middle line of the diagram equals the sum of the upper value and lower value.

23 - 1
Numbers in the segments of the upper left hand circle equal the product of the numbers in corresponding segments of the lower 2 circles, and the numbers in the segments of the upper right hand circle equal the sum of the numbers in corresponding segments of the bottom two circles.

24 - 12
Working from the bottom row to the apex of the triangle, the sum of the values in each row follows the sequence 15, 14, 13,12.

25 - K
Working through the diagram in columns, from top to bottom, letters move through the alphabet in steps of 5 for the left hand column, 7 for the next one, then 9, then 11.

26 - O
In each diagram, add the numerical values of the top 2 letters together, divide this by 2 and subtract 2 to give the numerical value of the lower letter.

27 - 6
Each row and column of the diagram adds up to 15.

28 - A
Split the diagram in half, horizontally and vertically, into quarters. Start in the top left cell of each quarter, and move around it in a clockwise spiral towards the centre. Letters are written in alternate segments, moving forward 7 letters at a time for the top left quarter, 6 letters for the top right, 5 letters for the lower right, and 4 letters for the lower left.

29 -   A:319
          B:424
In the first oval, the sum of the separate digits of each 3-digit number is 9, and in the second oval, the sum of the separate digits is 7.

30 - C
The sum of the numerical values of the letters in each column of the diagram equals 29.

SOLUTIONS

TEST 20

1 - U
The sum of the numerical values of the letters in opposite segments of the circle equals 26.

2 - J
Start with the letter J in the top left square, and move clockwise around the other squares. Letters follow the alphabetic sequence, skipping 4 letters at a time. Start with the X in the inner square in the top left, and move clockwise. These inner letters also follow the alphabetic sequence, skipping 5 letters at a time.

3 - 82
Start at the top and work down. Add the separate digits of the top number to the number itself to give the next one down, then subtract 12 to give the one after this. Continue with this alternating pattern.

4 - 4
In rows, from top to bottom, reading each pair of numbers as a 2-digit value, the numbers follow the sequence of square numbers, from 16 to 49, each written back to front.

5 - 1
In each row of the diagram, the values in the central circle equal the sums of the digits in corresponding segments of the left and right hand circles.

6 - D
Split the diagram horizontally into 3 rows, each 2 circles high. Start with the top left circle in each row, and move one space to the right, alternating down and up. Letters advance through the alphabet 5 letters at a time for the upper double row, 6 letters at a time for the central row, and 7 letters at a time for the bottom row.

7 - 2
Split the diagram into 3 vertical columns. The sum of the numbers in each column equal 17.

8 - X
Start at the top left and move to the right, then down one row and to the left etc in a snakes and ladders pattern. Letters advance through the alphabet 9 letters at a time.

9 - 31
As you move to the right, double the previous number and subtract 4, then 3, then 2, then 1 to give the next number along.

10 - 7
Start anywhere on the diagram, and move clockwise, calculating the sum of every third circle. This always equals 15.

11 - 5
In each circle, the digit is equal to the number of straight lines used to write the two letters in the same circle.

12 - 5
In each column of the diagram, the central value equals the average of the upper and lower numbers.

13 - B
Start with the J in the top left and move anti-clockwise around the shape in an hourglass shape. Letters advance through the alphabet in steps of 11 letters at a time.

14 - 14
In each star, the central value equals the sum of the top and lower two numbers, minus the left and right hand numbers.

15 - 1
Read each row of 3 numbers as a 3-digit number, and add the top row value to the middle row, to give the result written in the bottom row.

16 - O
Using the letters in the top right circle as a source, add 4 to the numerical values of each letter to give the letters in corresponding segments of the middle circle, and subtract 5 from the values to give the letters in corresponding segments of the bottom circle.

17 - 21
In each row, add the left and central numbers together, double it and add 1 to give the right hand value.

18 - F M R
Starting at the top and working down, add 5 to the numerical value of any even numbered letter, and add 7 to the numerical value of any odd numbered letter to give the letters in the space below.

19 - L
Starting with the letters in segments of the top left circle, add 3 to the numerical values of the letters, and write the results in the top right circle, with the relative positions of the letters moving 1/4 turn clockwise. Repeat this pattern, adding 4 to the values of the letters for the lower right hand circle, and adding 5 for the letters in the lower left hand circle, putting the results in the segments 1/4 turn clockwise each time.

20 - 73, 48
Starting at the top, add the left and right hand numbers together and subtract 5 to give the lower left number. Add 2 to the left hand number to give the lower right hand number.

21 - U
Starting at the top and working in diagonal lines from top right to bottom left, letters alternately increase in value by 9, then decrease by 3.

22 - 80
In each triangle, the central value equals the product of the 3 outer numbers subtracting the sum of the 3 outer numbers.

23 - Q
In each diagram, start with the letter in the top left and move clockwise around the others. Letters advance through the alphabet in steps given by the numerical value of the central letter.

24 - N
The sum of the numerical values of the letters around each star is always 55.

25 - I
Starting on the left, and moving along the diagram to the right, letters move through the alphabet in steps of 5, then 3, then 7, repeating this sequence.

26 - 9
In each triangle, multiply the lower two numbers together and add the upper number to give the value in the centre.

27 - C
In each circle, multiply the reverse alphabetical value of the upper left hand letter by the regular alphabetical value of the upper right hand letter to give the value in the lower segment.

28 - 5
Splitting the diagram in half both horizontally and vertically, each quarter contains a pattern of black squares, representing the letters W, X, Y and Z.

29 - 3
Using the lower two circles as a source, the values in corresponding segments of the upper left circle equal the sums of the numbers in the lower two circles. The values in the upper central circle equal the products of the values in the lower two circles, and the upper right circle equals the difference between values in the lower two circles.

30 - 6
Starting on the extreme left and right hand of the row and working towards the centre, add the end digits together and subtract 3 to give the next value along from the left, and add 1 to give the next value along from the right. Repeat this sequence, working towards the centre.